BIG REACTORS

BIG REACTORS

Practical Strategies for Parenting Highly Sensitive Children

CLAIRE LERNER, LCSW

BLOOMSBURY ACADEMIC
NEW YORK • LONDON • OXFORD • NEW DELHI • SYDNEY

BLOOMSBURY ACADEMIC
Bloomsbury Publishing Inc, 1359 Broadway, New York, NY 10018, USA
Bloomsbury Publishing Plc, 50 Bedford Square, London, WC1B 3DP, UK
Bloomsbury Publishing Ireland, 29 Earlsfort Terrace, Dublin 2, D02 AY28, Ireland

BLOOMSBURY, BLOOMSBURY ACADEMIC and the Diana logo are
trademarks of Bloomsbury Publishing Plc

First published in the United States of America 2025

Copyright © Bloomsbury Publishing, Inc., 2025

Cover image © istock/KyrychenkoAnastasiia

All rights reserved. No part of this publication may be: i) reproduced or transmitted in any form, electronic or mechanical, including photocopying, recording or by means of any information storage or retrieval system without prior permission in writing from the publishers; or ii) used or reproduced in any way for the training, development or operation of artificial intelligence (AI) technologies, including generative AI technologies. The rights holders expressly reserve this publication from the text and data mining exception as per Article 4(3) of the Digital Single Market Directive (EU) 2019/790.

Bloomsbury Publishing Inc does not have any control over, or responsibility for, any third-party websites referred to or in this book. All internet addresses given in this book were correct at the time of going to press. The author and publisher regret any inconvenience caused if addresses have changed or sites have ceased to exist, but can accept no responsibility for any such changes.

A catalog record for this book is available from the Library of Congress.

ISBN: HB: 979-8-88180-282-0
ePDF: 979-8-8818-5468-3
eBook: 979-8-88180-283-7

Typeset by Deanta Global Publishing Services, Chennai, India
Printed and bound in the United States of America

For product safety related questions contact productsafety@bloomsbury.com.

To find out more about our authors and books visit www.bloomsbury.com and sign up for our newsletters.

To all the amazing parents of deeply feeling kids. You deserve a heavy dose of validation and awe for the incredibly hard work you are doing to be the sensitive and loving moms and dads to your beautiful big reactors.

CONTENTS

Introduction 1

1 High Sensitivity: How It's Different from Sensory Processing Disorder, Attention-Deficit/Hyperactivity Disorder, Autism, and Anxiety 11

2 Intense Emotional and Sensory Reactivity 31

3 Inflexibility and Intense Need for Control 81

4 Anxiety 117

5 Cautious and Slow to Warm Up 137

6 Perfectionism, Sore Losing, Low Frustration, and Trouble Tolerating Corrections 167

7 Relationship Challenges with Siblings and Peers 193

8 Understanding and Addressing Other Common Issues 239

Closing Thoughts 263

Resources 264

Notes 268
References 273
Acknowledgments 276
Index 278
About the Author 281

Introduction

When I started providing parenting guidance to families of young children more than twenty years ago, a pattern quickly emerged. Almost all of the families who reached out for help had highly sensitive children (HSCs), sometimes called "spirited" or "deeply feeling" kids. They are more likely to have challenges regulating their big emotions because their brains are wired to process and react to their experiences in the world more deeply than other children. This translates into trouble adapting to everyday tasks and transitions. I call these kids "big reactors" because that is how their parents experience them.

My days are spent guiding parents of HSCs through the detective work of figuring out the root cause of their children's behavior and what approaches and strategies will help them thrive: to cooperate with necessary tasks, adapt to new people and situations, and form healthy relationships with family and friends.

It turns out that what works with these kids is not the popular, "positive" parenting strategies prevalent in social media, where most parents today seek information and guidance. This is especially true when it comes to "gentle parenting"—an approach that has gained tremendous popularity in the parenting universe in recent years and is touted as the gold standard for loving, responsive parenting.

Sarah Ockwell Smith,[1] who coined the concept, describes gentle parenting as an approach that is based on boundaries, empathy, understanding, and respect—all critically important factors that contribute to a strong, secure attachment that research has clearly shown results in the healthiest outcomes for children's social-emotional development over the long term.[2]

The problem is that, over time, "gentle parenting" has morphed into a permissive, prescriptive, one-size-fits-all approach with a dogma that doesn't work—and often backfires—with many big reactors. It dictates that parents must:

- *always* be engaged in loving, joyful connection with their children;
- have the power to and *always* be able to calm their children when they are upset—that if they appropriately "co-regulate" and "share their calm," their child will calm, too;
- *always* validate, process, and go deep into exploring feelings when their children are upset;
- *never* feel frustrated, angry, overwhelmed, or want a break from their children, because any separation, especially when children are distressed, is tantamount to neglect, even abandonment, and is an insensitive rejection of their feelings;
- *always* follow their children's lead, otherwise it sends the message that they don't care about or respect their children's needs and interests; and
- *always* be able to engage their children's cooperation, through empathy and giving them autonomy (read: endless choices),

giving directions or imposing limits to ensure an important task is done (toothbrushing, getting into a car seat) is seen as dictatorial and authoritarian.

These may be realistic expectations and strategies for the "dandelions"[3]—the adaptable, go-with-the-flow kids who are born with an "easy," flexible temperament; the kids who weather changes and transitions easily and cope with limits and life's natural disappointments and frustrations without a lot of distress or dysregulation.

But for parents of fierce and feisty big reactors, "gentle parenting"—as it is characterized in social media—rarely works. These are kids who go from zero to sixty in a nanosecond, often in reaction to seemingly minor events, such as their parents cutting their sandwich the wrong way, taking a different route home from school, paying *any* attention to the new baby, not letting them have more screen time, or not getting their blankets on exactly the way they want after twenty minutes of trying. When triggered into distress, these kids can have epic meltdowns that may be destructive—hitting, kicking, spitting, or hurling objects.

HSCs often reject calming tools. Or they can't access them in the heat of the moment, as one six-year-old explains: "I remember them [the calming tools] before. I remember them after. I just don't remember them in the middle." They don't like parents validating and talking about their emotions—it feels intrusive and overwhelming—and often respond with agitation and denial: "Stop talking to me! Stop telling me that! I am *not* sad!"

HSCs are not able to make healthy choices when their brains are flooded with big emotions. The more their parents try to convince them, or collaborate with them, to cooperate (as "gentle parenting" prescribes), the less likely they are to do so. They have a fierce need to exert control on the "outside" because they often feel out of control on the inside due to their deep and intense processing systems. Any demand or suggestion is seen as a threat to their autonomy, resulting in knee-jerk, defiant reactions. Time-ins, a primary "gentle parenting" strategy in which parents stay with children while they have meltdowns (versus time-outs, which entail a break between parent and child and thus, are taboo) are challenging and potentially unsafe when children have lost control of their bodies and are at risk of harming themselves or their parents.

One mom's lament so poignantly captures what hundreds of the parents I work with have shared:

> I am a total failure at this "gentle parenting" thing. My child rejects any and all calming tools. When I suggest she take deep belly breaths, she shouts back, "Stop telling me that!" When I validate her feelings, she shouts, "I am *not* angry!" I do all the things. I show empathy when she's having a hard time getting ready for school, but she doesn't get it together and get dressed, like Instagram says should miraculously happen. I read all about "sharing your calm" but no matter how calm I am, she rages. I fear that I am totally screwing up my kid because I don't seem to be able to be a "gentle parent."

These parents are sad and in despair over not being able to be the "gentle" parents they want to be. As hard as they try—and they try *very* hard—no matter how much empathy and validation they show, how calm they stay in the face of their children melting down, how many choices they offer so that their children feel respected and have agency, their kids still have major meltdowns and draw their parents into persistent power struggles. All are exhausted and depleted. Some are depressed.

After meeting, day after day, with parents of big reactors who feel alone and unable to find resources that meet them in their realities, I started contemplating writing a book that would fill this critical gap. But I am so busy seeing families all day long—my true passion and commitment—that I worried about diverting time from my clinical work to write another book.

Then, in February 2022, I wrote an article for *Psychology Today*, titled "Ten Traits of Highly Sensitive Children,"[4] that describes the key attributes and behaviors so many of the HSCs in my practice have in common. Within one week it had more than 1.6 million views. Since its publication, I have been inundated with emails from parents expressing deep appreciation for validating what they have experienced with their children, for helping them feel less alone and at sea, and for confirming that they don't have the only child who reacts in ways that feel extreme and irrational and that they are not abject failures. Many have shared stories of pediatricians and even mental health professionals dismissing their observations and concerns, not spending any time to explore the critical piece of the developmental puzzle that is temperament and offering popular parenting guidance that doesn't work with their kids and just makes them feel worse. The reaction to this article is what made it necessary for me to take the time to write this book—to share the insights I have gained about what makes these big reactors tick and the practical strategies that have worked for the hundreds of families I have been in the trenches with over the past few decades.

This book is also very personal to me. My son, Sam (now thirty-four), is an HSC. He was my first child, and I was a very anxious new mom. I couldn't tolerate any of his distress. I just wanted him to be happy, which I thought meant him *never* experiencing discomfort. That came to define my parenting approach and meant that anytime Sam was distressed, it was mom to the rescue. I mistakenly believed that struggling with a difficult task would result in low self-esteem, and so I rushed to fix all problems and prevent all frustration—whether it be placing a puzzle piece in its rightful place or solving a playground conflict. Anytime he had negative or difficult feelings, I was quick to cheerlead him out of them. I also failed to set limits in an attempt to avoid meltdowns and keep him "happy." My own distress at witnessing Sam struggle with life's expected challenges overrode my ability to see what he actually needed from me: to show him that I had total faith in his ability to cope with frustration and disappointment and that I had confidence in his ability to master the challenges he faced by giving him the space to work through a difficult task or experience. Trying to protect him from all discomfort became an obstacle to his learning to find his own solutions. But it's never too late. Over time, I saw the error of my ways, the disservice I was doing Sam, and I changed my approach. Sam is now a thriving adult despite my stint as a helicopter/lawnmower/snowplow (pick your poison/slur) parent. We share a very close and warm connection. His sensitivity has become his strength.

Another major motivator for writing this book is the research that shows that HSCs are more susceptible to both the detrimental effects of harsh environments and the benefits of positive and nurturing ones. This means that the caregiving HSCs experience has a deep impact, more so than on less sensitive children. When they have caregivers who tune in to and validate their feelings and experiences, who are able to provide the co-regulation these kids need—staying calm during their storms—and who support them in developing the tools they need to cope with and adapt to life's limits and expectations, it makes a big difference. At the same time, when HSCs have parents who are not sensitive or supportive, or who don't set the limits their kids need to develop the coping skills to manage their big emotions and reactions, they are more negatively affected than kids who are less sensitive.[5]

Often, when families come to see me, they have been struggling for years to make sense of their children and their big reactions. They despair at not being able to be the moms and dads they want to be, like Sally and Harlan, parents of six-year-old Brody. They sought consultation because Brody was being very defiant when he had to make a transition or follow a direction; for example, to stop watching TV and have breakfast, or to get his shoes on to go to school. He would get in their faces and angrily refuse or run and hide. Sometimes he became physically aggressive. They also described him as an amazing child: passionate, creative, and an "old soul"—wise well beyond his years. After a major meltdown, he once told them: "Sometimes my sad feelings get really big, and my love feelings get really small, and it scares me."

Sally and Harlan are great, loving parents, who, like most of the moms and dads who seek my consultation, were not prepared for a big reactor. The strategies they were using to get Brody to cooperate and to calm him when distressed weren't working. They felt terrible about the frustration and anger they were experiencing that Brody was clearly picking up on, as evidenced by drawings he made depicting his parents together, surrounded by a heart, while he was shown floating above them, outside of the heart, with his body crossed out. A second drawing showed his parents drawn quite large and himself very small. He was holding a square object, with tears running down his face. When his parents asked Brody about this drawing, he said it was about his sadness, and that the item in his hand was a pillow, which he was taking in case they made him leave the house.

I was able to help Sally and Harlan understand the root cause of Brody's big reactions and develop a set of tools to provide the compassion and support he needs while also setting the loving limits necessary to help him develop important coping skills. They hit the ground running and started to make course corrections immediately. At the next consult, they shared a new drawing Brody had made that reflected a very different internal self- and family representation. The symbolism was all about love: he was positioned between his mom and dad, holding their hands, and next to them were two hearts—one with "M D" written in it, for mom and dad; the one below it had a "B," for Brody. At the top of the page were the words, "I LOVE."

Harlan and Sally also reported that Brody's meltdowns were less frequent and intense and that he was finding ways to soothe himself and regroup. Telling him that he was a great kid having a hard time had really sunk in. Brody told them he repeats this to himself and that it helps him calm down. Of course, change doesn't always happen this instantaneously. However, most of my families do see progress fairly quickly because HSCs' experiences in the world affect them more deeply. Small changes can have a big impact.

ABOUT THIS BOOK

Chapter 1 focuses on how to differentiate between highly sensitivity children and those with disorders that have some overlap in attributes and behaviors: sensory processing disorder (SPD), attention-deficit/hyperactivity disorder (ADHD), autism spectrum disorder (ASD), and anxiety disorders.

The remaining chapters take in-depth looks at key attributes and behaviors of highly sensitive children that I consistently see in my work with families. Using cases from my practice, some of which are composites, I reveal the process through which I guide parents, teachers, and other caregivers to solve the challenges they struggle with. You will see that many of these attributes are interrelated. HSCs' deep processing of their experiences in the world—emotional and sensory—means that they are easily overwhelmed and, hence, have big reactions. Their keen self-awareness and awareness of others can make them quick to shame, more self-conscious, and prone to big, negative reactions to being corrected. Their intense need for control—to be sure things go the way they want and expect—is often at the root of many of the challenges they experience: trouble making transitions and adapting to new experiences, inflexibility, low frustration tolerance, perfectionism, difficulty losing, and, ultimately, increased anxiety when they can't control everything in their worlds.

There is not a chapter specifically devoted to discipline, because setting limits with love—teaching children how to manage their big emotions and cope with everyday tasks and routines—is addressed in every chapter. Establishing and holding boundaries in ways that are loving and supportive, rather than shaming, is especially important for helping big reactors learn self-regulation. Therefore, discipline concepts and strategies are embedded in almost every case in this book.

My first book, *Why Is My Child in Charge?* is not a prerequisite, but it may serve as a good companion to *Big Reactors*. It is a guide to parenting without power struggles—how to thread the sometimes seemingly elusive needle of being a loving, connected parent while also setting the clear limits and boundaries kids need to thrive. It provides detailed strategies for setting limits with love to help kids learn to manage not getting what they want when they want it when it comes to sleep, mealtimes, physical aggression, and other common challenges parents face, especially with big reactors.

While my work is based on and incorporates the science of early childhood and parenting—the focus of my more than twenty years at ZERO TO THREE—this book reflects my learnings from decades of consulting with parents, rather than formal research. As many of you may have found from your own exploration of the vast amount of parenting advice at your disposal, there is no one-size-fits-all approach. Just because a model shows efficacy in a study doesn't mean it will work for every child. What I am offering in this book are lessons learned about what works with big reactors based on my collaboration with thousands of families with HSCs in the hope that you will be able to apply some of these insights and tools to your own child and family. The insight from my own parenting journey—my (often painful) twenty-twenty hindsight—is also reflected in these pages.

Note: Throughout this book, I use "big reactor," "highly sensitive child," "HSC," and "deeply feeling child" interchangeably to describe these amazing and fierce kids.

1

High Sensitivity

How It's Different from Sensory Processing Disorder, Attention-Deficit/ Hyperactivity Disorder, Autism, and Anxiety

Our five-year-old, Gabriel, is a very bright, funny, charming little guy. But he still has a lot of tantrums that we thought would be over by this age. When he is happy, he is the most delightful child. But the second something doesn't happen exactly how or when he wants it, he is explosive. We are totally exhausted.

Gabriel is also very sensitive and self-conscious. He is easily offended. He doesn't like people focusing attention on or looking at him. During every school performance he has participated in, he turns his back from the audience. He is also a perfectionist and very self-critical when he doesn't do things perfectly.

Gabriel feels easily rejected. For example, the other morning I was giving his little sister a piggyback ride down the stairs. He went under his blankets and started screaming all sorts of inflammatory and threatening things because he wanted to go down the stairs first. When I try to talk to him about these incidents, he covers his ears. If we try to ignore his inappropriate language, he just escalates. He eventually calms down and feels bad about his behavior. Once the explosion is over, he will say things like, "I push people away, like Elsa (of Frozen)," or "My brain is so out of control—I don't know why I stay so mad."

Most parents who seek my services have a Gabriel. Whether the motivation to make that first call to me is intense and frequent tantrums, aggressive behavior, power struggles, sleep, or potty training, the common denominator is often that their child is highly sensitive.

WHAT IS HIGH SENSITIVITY?

High sensitivity (HS) is a temperament trait. Temperament refers to biologically based, consistent, enduring patterns of normative behavior, such as activity level, regularity of sleeping and eating, adaptability, intensity of emotion, mood, distractibility, persistence, attention span, and sensory sensitivity.[1] Temperament impacts how children take in or register, process, and act on their experiences in the world. It is something we are all born with, not something children choose or that parents instill. Temperament is not a disorder or a mental illness.[2]

Temperament helps us understand the "why" of children's behavior: why some children jump right into new situations and others are more hesitant and need time to warm up to the unfamiliar;

why some children go with the flow and weather life's ups and downs with ease and others have big reactions to seemingly minor events and transitions; why some children are more regulated in their sleeping and eating patterns, while others are more erratic; why some children have a very high activity level and others are more sedentary. It is also why siblings can be so different. They share DNA and grow up in the same family, but their reactions to the very same experiences—a move, a loss, their parents' approach to discipline—may be vastly different based on their temperament.

The scientific term for high sensitivity is sensory processing sensitivity (SPS), or "high environmental sensitivity."[3] It is a temperament trait characterized by increased awareness of, and sensitivity to, the environment. Highly sensitive people (HSPs) process sensory stimuli and information more strongly and deeply than others. Brain scans show that the parts of the brain associated with processing emotions and bodily sensations are more active in highly sensitive people.[4]

HSPs are sometimes referred to as "orchids"[5] because of how reactive they are to changes in their environment, just like the flower. In supportive and nurturing early environments, highly sensitive people have the capacity to flourish and may have better developmental trajectories than less sensitive individuals, just as orchids can reach extraordinary growth and beauty with the right care. In stressful and unsupportive early environments, highly sensitive children (HSCs) have poorer developmental outcomes and an increased likelihood of behavioral and psychological difficulties.[6]

Just as humans differ from one another on their level of activity, frustration tolerance, and other temperament traits, people also vary in how sensitive they are. Research shows sensitivity constitutes a continuum from low sensitivity to high sensitivity. It is estimated that around 30 percent of the population is highly sensitive, or "orchids." "Tulips," or people who are moderately sensitive, make up 40 percent; and 30 percent are low-sensitive individuals, or "dandelions"—named for the plant that can thrive in even harsh environments.[7]

It is thought that HSPs are critical for the survival of our human species. Their keen attunement to environmental cues and their "pause to check system"[8] alerts them to danger and enables thoughtful, smart decision-making. Dr. Elaine Aron, a highly respected psychologist, posits (and others agree) that "being highly sensitive has evolutionary value by fostering survival strategies through careful observation and deliberation before acting. Research suggests that a population balance between more sensitive individuals and less sensitive individuals creates an adaptive advantage under different environmental conditions."[9] In short, evolution would not allow as much as 30 percent of the population to have a trait that did not have an important role in our survival as a species.

TYPICAL CHARACTERISITCS OF HIGHLY SENSITIVE CHILDREN

Deep Processing

HSCs are deep thinkers and, thus, are unusually insightful. They keenly focus on and analyze seemingly everything. It's as if their brains never turn off. Parents often describe their HSCs as "old souls."

They often share profound insights and ask deep, existential questions starting from a very young age. They have tremendous capacity for empathy as they adeptly tune in to people and pick up on and react to the moods of others. Typical stories from parents of HSCs include:

- "Sasha [five] picks up on everything. She notices the second the tone changes between me and Mitchell (my husband) and will try to intervene. She gets between us and commands: 'Stop this right now! No more talking! Daddy, you need to kiss mommy.'"
- "During the winter holidays, Reuben [three] proclaimed: 'I don't like Santa. He keeps asking me if I've been naughty or nice. I can't be good all the time—that's impossible. I like Baby Jesus and Chanukah. They don't ask me if I'm good.'" This, from a person who has just been learning about the world for not much more than thirty-six months!
- "We told Lucca, after my sister died, that she was in a better place. He asked: 'If Auntie is in a better place, why don't we all go there?'"

When my highly sensitive son, Sam, was four, I took him and three friends to see *The Lion King*. At the end of the movie, Sam was sobbing while his buddies were just super excited. They had focused on the adventure aspects of the story. Sam, on the other hand, homed in on the fact that Simba felt responsible for his father's death. Trying to make sense of this disturbing content was overwhelming his four-year-old brain, which had no way to logically process this complex information. It left him flooded with emotions he could not make sense of. His friends, on the other hand, were oblivious. They reacted to it as an action-adventure movie and were not burdened by the weight of the disturbing content that Sam had so intensely absorbed.

Profound Empathy

Being so tuned in to others makes HSCs very empathetic. They are often the first to comfort a person or animal in distress. They pick up on and respond to the nonverbal communications of others. As one mom explains: "Henry has the superpower of tuning in to how other people feel before they even know it." Another child, who saw his mom crying, told her he was going to make her a happy card that she can open when she is feeling sad to make it all better.

Big Emotional Reactions, Both Positive and Negative

HSCs' intensity means they may live at the extremes. Their parents often describe them as either ecstatic or enraged, with no middle register. They either are on top of the world or everything is terrible. Their emotions can fluctuate very quickly. Like Shayla, who, after a wonderful day with hours of fun and joy, announced at bedtime that "this is the worst day ever!" when her dad said "no" to going back downstairs (once she was already in bed with the lights out). She insisted she needed to check on a block structure she had been working on earlier that day. The intensity and unpredictability of their emotions can be overwhelming and result in more frequent and intense meltdowns.

Cautious and "Slow to Warm Up" to New People and Experiences

Because HSCs are such deep processors, they need time to adjust and feel comfortable in novel situations, engaging their "pause to check system." When they enter a new situation—be it a classroom, a birthday party, or swim class—their wheels are turning. They wonder: What is this place? What will happen here? Who are these people? What can I expect from them? Will they like me? Will I be safe? Will I be good at whatever is expected of me here?

To cope, they may fiercely cling to their comfort zone and resist engaging in anything new. They tend to have a harder time separating from their parents. It takes them longer to adapt when they start childcare or preschool. They refuse to go to soccer or swimming, even when they love these activities. But with support and scaffolding, HSCs are often able to move through the discomfort and thrive.

Prone to Anxiety and Fears

The deep thinking and constant analysis of their environment makes HSCs extremely bright and insightful. Their brains never turn off as they try to make sense of and cope with all the information they are taking in. But given their limited real-world perspective and experience, some of this information is impossible to process and make sense of, which results in anxiety over what they can't understand or control. Their cognitive processing is way ahead of their emotional maturity. For example:

- A three-year-old refuses to take a bath after seeing an episode of a TV show in which a bathtub overflows and floods the house.

- A four-year-old demands to be carried—he won't walk on the floor—after seeing the movie *Moana* and worries the floor will turn into lava.

- A six-year-old fights sleep at night after a friend told him his grandma had died, which meant she was "asleep."

- For several weeks after seeing *The Lion King*, Sam was very clingy to his dad; he wouldn't let him out of his sight. He also had a sleep regression.

As you can see, HSCs' depth of processing means that they often experience more anxiety than children who are less sensitive.

Negative Mood and Pessimistic Outlook

HSCs' deep thinking and analysis results in a lot of "what-ifs?" and worry that can take them to dark places. They feel overwhelmed on the inside because they don't have an "off" button; their brains are constantly working, trying to make sense of all they are processing. To cope, they try to control whatever they can on the outside. Thinking twenty steps ahead ensures they will be prepared for anything—to feel in control of all potential outcomes. Preparing for the worst protects them from disappointment but can also lead to a bleak outlook, as evidenced by proclamations like:

- "I'm never going to be able to make it" (across the monkey bars).

- "We're never going to find it!" (the missing puzzle piece).
- "I'm never going to make friends at the new school. Nobody is going to like me."

Strong Sense of Self-Awareness

Parents of HSCs frequently share profound statements their children make that reveal their deep self-reflection.

- A six-year-old says to his dad after an epic meltdown: "Remember when I said that mean thing to you yesterday when I was mad? I was lying. I just wanted to make you feel bad, too."
- A five-year-old told her mom after she ran upstairs and shut herself in her room, "I was so mad that you were playing the game with Theo that I thought was our special game. I think you love him more."
- A four-year-old tells his mom after he tried to hit her: "Sometimes my brain gets all crazy and crunchy and I can't get the monster out of my head."

Self-Conscious and Quick to Feel Shame

HSCs tend to be quick to feel shame when they can't do something perfectly immediately, or when they have made a mistake or done something wrong. Accordingly, seemingly benign corrections or suggestions—how to hold scissors correctly, how to aim the ball to get it in the basket, how to solve a problem with a peer—are experienced as criticisms or personal indictments, not as helpful guidance. They react negatively, and sometimes explosively, to being corrected. They get angry and defensive, cover their ears, run away, or completely shut down when faced with an adult who is trying to instruct them in some way.

HSCs may also become preoccupied with how others see them. They get very uncomfortable when any attention is called to them, even when parents or other adults are saying complimentary things. They are sensitive to feeling judged. That's why they are particularly uncomfortable with praise—as counterintuitive as that may seem. They know this means they are being evaluated and react negatively to the pressure. This is also why some HSCs are prone to perfectionism. When they can't do something exactly as their brain is telling them it should be, they feel ashamed and experience it as a loss of control, which is very uncomfortable and hard to tolerate.

Highly Creative

Because they process input from the sensory world so deeply, HSCs perceive more intensely. They have a heightened awareness of details in nature, art, music, and everyday life. One child, who is now an accomplished artist, tried to express to her mom, starting at age three, how deeply she experienced colors. This enhanced perception can fuel the creative process by offering more material for inspiration. HSCs' deep processing of emotions, their rich inner lives, and their intense imaginations provide endless fodder for weaving elaborate stories, drawing/painting, and other creative endeavors.

Inflexible and Controlling

Because HSCs register their feelings and experiences in the world so deeply, they live in a state of high alert to prepare for and protect themselves from whatever big emotion or event they may be exposed to next that may feel overwhelming or uncomfortable. To cope, they come up with fixed ideas and expectations about how things should be to make daily life more manageable. This makes them inflexible—unable to accept an alternative way of doing things. They may dictate where people will sit, how loud the music can be, what color bowl their cereal should come in, what clothes they will and will not wear, or how close the chicken can be to the carrots on their dinner plate. These seemingly irrational demands are all coping mechanisms HSCs use to control an environment that otherwise feels out of control. The more out of control these kids feel on the inside, the more controlling they become on the outside.

Difficulty with Change, Transitions, and Unexpected or Unpredictable Events

Because of their strong need for control, HSCs often resist and get very dysregulated when they have to make a change, like going from home to an activity (even when they love it once they get engaged in it) or when something unexpected happens, like mom coming to school pick-up when they expected grandma.

All these traits add up to HSCs developing a host of coping mechanisms to try to gain control of a world that, a lot of the time, feels like too much to manage. This can lead to a range of challenges that, while not exclusive to HSCs, occur more frequently and with greater intensity for them.

DIFFERENCES BETWEEN SENSORY PROCESSING SENSITIVITY AND SENSORY PROCESSING DISORDER

SPS (same as HS, high sensitivity) is sometimes confused with sensory processing disorder (SPD).[10] While there is overlap in behaviors of HSCs and kids with SPD in that they both can have big reactions to sensory input, they are distinct phenomena. SPS is a temperament trait, not a disorder. A disorder is defined as a clinically significant disturbance in an individual's cognition, emotional regulation, or behavior that takes them off track in their development and affects their daily functioning.[11] Children who are highly sensitive may have a more pronounced response to sensory stimuli than others. They may need more time and space to process and recover from intense or overwhelming experiences. An HSC may feel anxious or overstimulated in a noisy, crowded environment, or may be deeply affected by a sad or violent scene in a movie, but with support from a trusted caregiver who helps them make sense of their experiences and reactions, they don't get stuck and can recover and move on.

Sensory processing disorder, on the other hand, is a neurological disorder (or form of neurodivergence) characterized by difficulties in processing and responding to sensory information from the environment. While SPS involves deeply processing sensory input, it is not the same as being unable to fully process it.[12]

SPD involves atypical patterns of how the brain processes sensory information, often resulting in heightened or diminished responses to sensory stimuli, such as touch, sound, taste, or smell. Some researchers have theorized that SPD may be linked to a hyperconnected or hyperresponsive neural network in specific sensory regions of the brain. Symptoms may include sensory-seeking or sensory-avoiding behaviors, difficulty with sensory modulation, sensory-related anxiety, sensory shutdowns, and sensory meltdowns.[13]

HSCs may have strong reactions to sounds or textures and be particular about food and clothing, but with support and changes to the environment, they can adapt. For example, a three-year-old I worked with insisted on wearing Crocs twenty-four seven. Then one day, when it was time to get ready to go to school, his dad realized they were caked in dirt from a muddy visit to the playground the previous day, so this child had to wear a different pair of shoes. He was very upset and refused. His dad calmly helped him to the car, secured sneakers on him, and by the time they got to school the child had adapted.

For a child with SPD, their systems are not accurately processing the sensory input, and so environmental supports are often not sufficient to help them adapt. Faced with the same situation as the child with the Crocs, children with SPD may not as easily adapt, may stay distressed longer, and may ultimately keep taking the sneakers off. Their challenges with sensory processing can lead to significant difficulties in everyday activities and social interactions and require therapeutic intervention with an occupational therapist. It's important to note that while SPS and SPD are distinct phenomena, some HSCs I see also have SPD. So, if you have a child whose reaction to sensory input is interfering in daily functioning, I strongly recommend getting an occupational therapy evaluation to determine whether SPD is a factor in your child's behavior.

DIFFERENCES BETWEEN SENSORY PROCESSING SENSITIVITY AND ATTENTION-DEFICIT/HYPERACTIVY DISORDER

While sensory processing sensitivity and attention-deficit/hyperactivity disorder (ADHD) overlap in some ways, they are distinct phenomena. ADHD is a neuropsychiatric disorder, not a temperament trait.[14] They are both characterized by emotional reactivity, propensity for overstimulation, and anxiety. Both may cause difficulty focusing and overstimulation. But the root cause is different. For HSCs it is often due to being overwhelmed by emotional and sensory input that diverts them from being able to stay focused and on task. For children with ADHD, the root cause is a challenge with executive functioning, impulse control, and/or hyperactivity. While both groups may exhibit emotional sensitivity, HSCs may be more empathetic and emotionally responsive to others, while children with ADHD may struggle with peer relationships due to impulsivity.

Children with ADHD are more likely to react impulsively in a highly stimulating environment, while HSCs are more likely to pause and reflect before acting. Children with ADHD have a harder time sitting still and tend to be more impulsive than HSCs—they may call out repeatedly during a group time at school and have a difficult time finishing projects.

Brain scans show differences between brains with ADHD and brains with SPS.[15] ADHD is associated with less activation in areas of the brain involved in cognitive processing that impact self-regulation, attention, and inhibition. Scans of people with SPS show more activation in these areas, as well as those related to depth of processing and empathy.

If you are concerned about ADHD, it's important to consult with a child development expert to identify the root cause of your child's challenges and determine the best path to helping them thrive.

DIFFERENCES BETWEEN HIGH SENSITIVITY AND AUTISM SPECTRUM DISORDER

High sensitivity (HS) is often confused with autism spectrum disorder (ASD) as there is some overlap in symptoms: both groups are affected by how their systems perceive and process sensory information from their environment; both tend to get overwhelmed by environmental stimuli, including sensitivity to noise, light, touch, and other sensory input; both also exhibit strong emotional reactions and struggle with transitions and adapting to new environments. As a result, HSCs and children with ASD may have more frequent meltdowns, have an outsize need to be in control, be inflexible, and resist transitions and change. But they are distinct phenomena and require different approaches to diagnosis and management.

ASD is a neurobiological disorder characterized by a range of challenges in social interaction, communication, and behavior. It is a lifelong neurodevelopmental divergence present in around 2 percent of the population. The disorder impacts other areas of functioning not specific to sensory processing. Being highly sensitive is a temperament trait and not a disorder.[16]

ASD presents differently in each individual, leading to the term "spectrum." The *DSM-5* (*Diagnostic and Statistical Manual*, fifth edition) now identifies three levels of ASD to describe the "spectrum."[17] Children diagnosed with level 1 tend to be "high-functioning" and able to engage and participate in typical daily routines and activities with some support. Children with level 2 are more affected and require greater support in academic and social settings. Children with level 3 need intensive support. ASD is a diagnosable condition that is typically identified in childhood, although some people may not receive a diagnosis until later in life.

Differences in the Brain

Dr. Bianca Acevedo of the University of California's Neuroscience Research Institute analyzed twenty-seven research papers comparing high sensitivity, autism, and other conditions and found that there are neurological differences between HSPs (highly sensitive people) and those with ASD. Brain scans of HSPs show higher-than-normal levels of activity in areas that are involved with empathy, social processing, and reflective thinking—meaning, relevant information may take longer to process and feel more intense. HSPs show more activity in their mirror neuron system: when watching someone else do or feel something, their neurons fire as if they were doing or feeling the same thing. In contrast, the brains of those on the autistic spectrum tend to be less active when it comes to those regions related to calmness, self-control, emotional regulation, and the ability to self-reflect.[18]

Differences in Behavior

Note: these differences will vary based on the level of the child's ASD and where on the continuum of sensitivity an HSC is.

Self-Regulation

HSCs' heightened emotional and sensory sensitivity often leads to a greater awareness of their emotional and physical states. This enables them to ultimately know themselves and use this information to help them adapt. If they go to a playground and discover that their favorite slide is being repaired and not in use, they may be very disappointed and melt down, but with time and encouragement from an adult they are able to adapt and explore other equipment.

Children with ASD are both over (hyper) and under (hypo) reactive to sensory input and have a hard time decoding it. Rather than processing this input in a way that helps them understand and navigate the world, it can impede that ability. They may have difficulty identifying where to focus their attention. They may find shoes as important as a person's face.[19]

Because children with ASD also struggle to understand and communicate their emotions and needs, it makes it more challenging to regulate their responses. When they confront something unexpected, or a disappointment, their distress may last longer and they may not be able to choose another option.

Social Communication

HSCs are often excellent social communicators—adept at expressing their feelings and making deep connections with others. They gain meaning from interacting with the world around them. They are known for their keen insight into others' social cues and hyperawareness of what is going on for others around them. This helps them ultimately develop a "theory of mind"—a very important cognitive skill that enables children to recognize that other people's thoughts and feelings may be different from their own; that while they may want the block structure to be for dinosaurs, another child may want it to be for farm animals.

Children with ASD may have difficulty mastering this "theory of mind" (depending on where they are on the spectrum). They often struggle with making eye contact, recognizing faces, accurately interpreting social cues, and decoding the emotions and intentions of others, which leads to misunderstandings and challenges in conveying their thoughts and emotions and getting along with others. Children with ASD often react in ways that are not contingent or responsive to the signals of those they are interacting with, which makes social interactions confusing and, thus, more stressful and less rewarding.

When an HSC knocks down another child's tower, they may react with shame at having done something harmful. They may cover their ears or even laugh due to their discomfort at being corrected because they know they have done something wrong. A child with ASD in the same situation may not accurately process the other child's emotions and thus, not show any awareness about or discomfort at having done something harmful. They may just keep on playing.

Intensity of Focus

HSCs may intensely focus on ideas and activities that are captivating to them but have a broad range of interests. Children with ASD have a more narrow and specific set of interests or preoccupations that can become repetitive and compulsive, to the exclusion of other activities. This behavior is often observed from a young age.

Self-Stimulation/Soothing

Children with ASD often engage in self-soothing behaviors that regulate their systems—making repetitive movements (referred to as "stimming") and sounds, and ritualistic behaviors that are not characteristic of HSCs.

Need for Predictability

While both HSCs and children with ASD crave and thrive on sameness and predictability, HSCs are better able to adapt to change with adult support, such as helping kids anticipate what to expect in new situations and offering a range of calming tools they can use when they are distressed. Children with ASD tend to have a more difficult time adapting and require more intensive support.

DIFFERENCES BETWEEN HIGH SENSITIVITY AND ANXIETY DISORDERS

While HSCs tend to experience more anxiety than less sensitive children, it doesn't necessarily mean your highly sensitive child has developed or will develop an anxiety disorder. It's a matter of how affected your child is by their worries and fears. If, with support, they are able to work through the anxiety and it's not interfering in their daily functioning—meaning they are able to participate in their developmentally appropriate activities and tasks—then it's not considered a disorder.

If the anxiety is negatively affecting your child's daily functioning—they are refusing to go to school, they won't participate in any activities outside the home, they're having trouble eating or sleeping, or it's impacting their ability to take pleasure in their experiences in the world—it is important to seek professional guidance to make an accurate assessment and get the help you need to best support your child.

FINAL THOUGHTS

HSCs may also have SPD, ADHD, ASD, or anxiety. If you have any concerns about your child's behavior, seek help from your pediatrician or another trusted child development expert who can guide you through the assessment process. It's also important to note that while being highly sensitive is not a disorder, many HSCs have challenges routine expectations and challenges and require special support from their primary caregivers to help them learn to manage their big reactions. This book addresses these challenges and how to lovingly support HSCs.

SPD, ADHD, and ASD are complex neurological, brain-based disorders that I have described in the most general ways. To learn more about these conditions, see the appendix.

2

Intense Emotional and Sensory Reactivity

From day one, I noticed that Mireille [five] had very big reactions. She was just extra . . . about everything. She was hyper tuned in; she noticed and reacted to everything. She would fuss if I changed the lighting or moved rooms. She hated being changed. If I turned my attention away for even one second, she would cry. She seemed from a very early age to know that I was her person and wouldn't go to anyone else.

She has grown into an incredible person. She is such a deep thinker and is so creative. The other day we were at the beach. She was looking at the ocean and said, "Mom, those waves are grandma and grandpa coming back for a visit and to tell us they are fine." Adults absolutely adore her. She talks and engages like a sophisticated grown-up. But she has a hard time with kids because her feelings get hurt easily. She gets so overwhelmed by and focused on her feelings that she gets stuck. This can lead to tantrums that sometimes last more than an hour. I am so ashamed to admit this—it's a terrible way to feel about your child—but I feel suffocated and totally burnt out. I don't know how to be the mom she needs me to be.

Highly sensitive children (HSCs) notice, absorb, and analyze everything. They pick up on subtle nuances and meanings that less-sensitive children may not register. This makes HSCs incredibly bright, empathetic, and insightful. They often ask very deep, philosophical questions about complex, existential phenomena starting at an early age. I frequently hear stories from parents about how they can't let their children watch emotionally charged content because of the distress it causes, like my son Sam's intense and intuitive reaction to *The Lion King*. If the villain has a beard, they become fearful of men they see out in the world with facial hair. If a mother dies in a movie, they become clingy to their moms and get preoccupied with and stressed over the concept of death.

One mom articulated what many parents of big reactors feel: "I think this is the most exhausting part of having an HSC—not knowing what will throw him and turn our day into chaos. Our little guy was happily watching a mountain biking reel with his dad when he burst into tears. Through the sobbing he told us that he was never going to see that bike trail because it's in Canada and he never wants to leave Australia." I still have the most vivid memory of Sam, when he was about four, approaching me as I was doing dishes at the sink—my back to him. He asked why I was sad. I had just received some upsetting news, but I wasn't crying or showing any outward emotion (or so I thought). He couldn't even see my face. He just "read" my body language and sensed my emotions.

While this depth of processing can be an amazing attribute, it can also overwhelm children whose cognitive processing is beyond their emotional capacity to make sense of everything they are taking in. They don't have the life experience to put things into perspective.

When their brains are flooded with thoughts and feelings they can't fully understand, it results in big reactions, often meltdowns. This can be exhausting for them and for their parents.

IMPACTS OF SENSORY PROCESSING

HSCs' deep processing extends to the sensory world. Big reactors may register what they see, hear, feel, taste, and smell more intensely. This can increase children's discomfort, making them more irritable and prone to meltdowns. This also explains their seemingly outsize, irrational reactions to typical life experiences. They may become afraid of public bathrooms because the flusher is too jarring and loud. They may reject foods that have strong tastes and smells. They may find bright lights uncomfortable. They may refuse to go to swim class to avoid getting splashed in the face or, worse, having to dunk their head underwater. They may have seemingly outsize reactions to minor booboos. "Our six-year-old bumped her shoulder against the door frame and reacted as if a Mack Truck had hit her. She complained about it all day, demanding medicine and compresses."

Children whose systems naturally regulate and adapt to sensory input are more flexible, unhampered by the range of sensations they experience. While the first few days at preschool may feel overwhelming, their brains quickly habituate to, and get comfortable with, all the sounds, the high activity level, and the frequent transitions and they are good to go. Highly sensitive children may need more time and support to feel comfortable in a new, highly stimulating environment.

Jessie (three) is a slow-to-warm-up child who can get overwhelmed in environments that are loud and chaotic. She began refusing to go to birthday parties because the inevitable, sudden, loud outburst of the "Happy Birthday!" song was so overwhelming to her. She also started to fear candles because of the association she had made with these uncomfortable situations. Her parents could have just stopped taking her to birthday parties, but they knew that would mean Jessie missing out on important social experiences and wouldn't help her learn to cope with discomfort—a fact of life. Instead, they find out in advance when the cake is going to be served. They give Jessie the choice to put headphones on or to go into a different room until the candles are blown out. Jessie now goes to parties more willingly and finds them much more pleasurable.

Threading this needle of supporting versus enabling your big reactor requires getting clear on what your child needs versus what they want or what is comfortable for them. It starts with getting clear on your role, which brings me to the common phenomenon in families with HSCs—the emotional support parent (ESP).

WHEN YOU ARE YOUR CHILD'S EMOTIONAL SUPPORT PARENT

The emotional support parent (ESP) is a term that a client, who is her child's primary and most desired (and demanded) source of comfort, used to describe herself. It took my breath away because it so perfectly captures the experience of so many of the parents (most often moms) I work with who have big reactors. They are highly tuned in to their kids, keenly focused on anticipating anything that might cause them stress and tirelessly working to head it off. Not to mention what an apt acronym, given that ESPs often have extrasensory perception about their kids.

If you are an ESP, you know the drill; you are working twenty-four seven to head off the tantrums that can be fierce and very distressing to the whole family system: making sure the pair of pants your child will wear are clean every morning; preparing their food to ensure there is nothing foreign they aren't expecting (like a stray poppy seed that found its way onto their plain bagel); going through the plan for the next day six times before lights-out and ensuring there is no divergence from it. ESPs often feel like they are the only one who truly understands and knows how to comfort their child and get them through the myriad difficult moments as they navigate daily life. I feel you. I am a recovering ESP.

Being your child's ESP is often complicated. You may thrive on the deep connection you share with your child and the important role you are playing as your child's primary source of comfort. If you are like many ESPs, you are often the preferred parent, which can be a double-edged sword. On the one hand it feels great to be so needed—to know that your child trusts you so completely and that you are their person.

At the same time, many ESPs struggle with feelings of resentment about being the only one who can take their child to the bathroom, cut their sandwich, put them to bed at night, and calm them. This takes enormous patience and physical and emotional energy. As Marguerite explains: "I love the deep closeness we share. But I also feel suffocated, like my daughter is feeling at me and that she wants to control my every movement. I am overwhelmed and exhausted.

When I am being honest with myself, I feel resentful and angry toward her which feels horrible. I don't know how to give her what she needs without feeling like the life is being sucked out of me. I am not a bottomless pit of empathy."

As it turns out, the ESP is not just the most desired and demanded source of comfort. You also might find yourself being blamed when anything goes wrong. Since you are their person—the one they trust to have their back, to keep them safe and secure—this also means that you should be able to solve all their problems and prevent all pain. So, when something unexpected or unwanted happens, you are not just the cause, you are responsible for making it all better:

- "Levi is desperate for me. He sticks to me like Velcro. He wants me to do everything for him. I am the only one who can help him. But I am also the fuel for his fire. When he is upset, because something has gone wrong that I have absolutely nothing to do with—like his banana breaking in half—I am the target of his anger and am to blame."

- "Scarlett drops pizza on the floor, I'm responsible. I get a drip of water from her toothbrush on her shirt—I did it on purpose. She falls off her scooter, I made it happen. And, according to her, I should never have bought the scooter—that she had begged for!—in the first place. Don't I know that she *hates* scooters?"

Recently, I met with a couple, Celia and Dori, who have a three-year-old named Addie. Celia, the ESP, shares that she's having very negative feelings about Addie, which is causing her horrible guilt.

Addie insists that Celia do everything for her. She can't get a break. She is annoyed all the time with Addie and Celia knows Addie is picking up on it, asking her over and over: "Is mommy sad? Mad?" At this point, Celia's wife, Dori, chimes in with a story of how differently she and Celia approach playground visits with Addie. Celia is always within arm's reach of Addie, constantly scaffolding her experience and instantaneously solving whatever problem may arise. Dori has a very different relationship with Addie. She hangs back more and gives Addie space to figure things out on her own. Addie functions more independently with Dori.

Through this discussion, Celia sees that she has set up certain expectations with Addie that are resulting in her being much more dependent on Celia. Celia shares that she is a highly sensitive person and did not get her emotional needs met as a child. There was no acknowledgment of feelings and she felt very alone. She identifies strongly with Addie as an HSC and is fiercely committed to Addie knowing she is loved and that *all* of her feelings matter. She misinterprets Addie's struggle when she faces a challenge or doesn't like a limit as being harmful to her. This makes it hard for Celia to resist jumping in to rescue Addie when she faces a challenge. It's also hard to set limits because of the major meltdowns that ensue when Addie doesn't get what she wants, which are very triggering to Celia.

This describes a very common dynamic I see in families. Often, the parent who is not the ESP reports that when the ESP isn't present, the child is much more regulated, cooperative, and resilient. When the ESP is around, the child acts more helpless, needier, and less competent. Why? Kids are constantly trying to figure out what the expectations are in any given situation and then they adapt to those expectations—be it with parents, teachers, grandparents, nannies, or other caregivers. That is why the same child can behave so differently depending on who is in charge.

HSCs know their ESP is very focused on and tuned in to their feelings; that the ESP is the person who goes deep with them, who makes space for all of their feelings, which is essential and beautiful. HSCs are often clever and strategic. They become masters at pulling at their ESP's heartstrings to get what they want, saying things like: "But mommy, that makes me so sad when you won't lie down with me longer (at bedtime). I haven't had enough time with you today." They know there is no way their ESP can say "no" to talking about feelings, and that maybe that will lead to extending bedtime, delay leaving for school, avoid putting away toys—or any of the many tasks or transitions kids are not keen on and will try to put off, if possible.

Children know their ESP is always there to troubleshoot, so they come to expect and rely on it. Children rise to a higher level of functioning and independence with other adults who give them wider berth and don't jump in to do for them things they can do for themselves. Children also tend to put up less of a fight and be more cooperative with the parent and other caregivers who are clearer and more consistent with limit-setting. This doesn't mean these adults are cold, harsh, or punitive and that the child is cooperating out of fear. These caregivers are being authoritative, not authoritarian. If, at the end of their loving bedtime routine, the child says they have one more thing to talk about, this parent is comfortable saying: "I know you have so much to share, and I can't wait to hear about it in the morning. Now it's time for sleep. I love you and can't wait to see you when your wake-up light comes on."

These kids are not being manipulative. There is nothing wrong with: wanting more time with a parent, trying to derail an unwanted limit from being set, or trying to avoid discomfort. That's human nature. Kids will rely on whatever works to get what they want or to fend off what they don't want. The question is whether what they want is what they need—what is best for them—in that moment.

That's why figuring out how to support versus enable your HSC is so important. I hope the mindshifts and stories that follow help you find that sweet spot where you can make a deep connection with your child while also setting the important limits that are essential for your child's individuation and healthy, independent functioning far into the future.

MINDSHIFTS

There are some very important foundational shifts in perspective that enable parents to help their fierce kids learn to manage their big emotions and reactions. They are especially important if you are an ESP.

My child is not overreacting on purpose. You have an amazing child whose system so deeply processes their experiences in the world that they get overwhelmed and are triggered into discomfort more easily. *They are not being overly dramatic, purposefully losing it, misbehaving, or trying to humiliate you. They are not manipulative; they are demanding and controlling because they are desperately trying to manage a world that can feel overwhelming.* They need your help to learn to cope effectively with their big feelings.

My child is not being hurtful, with their words or their bodies, on purpose. Big reactors are known to go from zero to sixty in a nanosecond. When triggered into discomfort, their "downstairs brain"[1]—the primitive, reactive, part of the brain—takes over. In these moments, kids can say a lot of horrible and shocking things and lose control of their bodies—hitting, kicking, spitting, and/or biting. They are not acting with premeditation and purpose. *They are great kids having a difficult moment.*

I know this may be confusing; it seems intentional when your five-year-old hurls a toy across the room in frustration or tells you they hate you and want you to leave the house and never come back. They are not planning these actions; they are purging their pain. They don't *want* to be harmful. This mindshift is so important because when you take it personally, or see your child's behavior as malicious and intentional, you are more likely to react harshly and punitively, which usually escalates the out-of-control behavior. Children internalize that they are vicious and violent and the powerful, self-fulfilling prophecy prevails.

My child's big feelings are not harmful to them. Many parents of big reactors, especially ESPs, worry that the intensity of their children's feelings and the level of distress they experience and express when they are overwhelmed is inherently harmful. This results in parents working very hard to avoid situations or setting limits that may trigger their child. When their child melts down, they rush to try to make it all better, which is rarely helpful and often impossible.

The mindshift to make is that *feelings are not harmful—they are part of being human*. Helping children learn to process and make sense of their feelings is critical. When you accept your child's emotions, guide them to explore and understand these feelings, and help them develop effective coping tools and strategies, they learn to manage their big feelings in healthy ways, which leads to the next mindshift.

My child needs me to validate, not try to talk them out of, their feelings. We love our children so deeply and want them to be happy. So, when they share difficult or uncomfortable feelings, our knee-jerk reaction is to try to change their feelings by minimizing or talking them out of their emotions: "Don't say you're stupid! You are the smartest kid I know." "You are going to love the new school—it has a bigger playground!" We want to make the uncomfortable feelings (for them and us) go away. We fear that acknowledging them amplifies them. But ignoring or minimizing feelings doesn't make them magically disappear. In fact, without a healthy opportunity for expression, feelings get acted out, which can lead to more, not less, stress for your child . . . and you.

My child needs me to be empathetic to, but not take on, their feelings. This is easier said than done, especially if you are an ESP, as we tend to *feel* our children's pain. When our child is sad, we feel down. When our child is anxious, we absorb and experience their anxiety. This *enmeshment* can be exacerbated when, as one mom put it, "He's hitting me with one hand and pulling me with the other! Feel as bad as I do . . . *and* make me feel better." It's a basic human need to feel understood and not alone. For HSCs, this need is particularly strong. They want someone else to feel their pain and that someone is you, the ESP.

But *merging* with our children in this way can be exhausting and make it hard to be the rock our kids need us to be when they are distressed and dysregulated. They get rejected by a group at the playground and we feel sick to our stomachs. When our child loses it because their block tower keeps falling down, we kinesthetically experience their frustration and need to make it go away by rebuilding the structure for them. When we internalize our children's feelings and act on them, they sense it. This tends to amplify, not reduce, their distress and ultimately becomes an obstacle to their learning to manage those emotions. Our agitation increases theirs.

When my daughter, Jess, was seven, she went through a period when she woke up really cranky and out of sorts. She begged not to go to school. I went straight to catastrophizing (as we ESPs are known to do): Was she depressed? Would she become a school-refuser? Not to minimize or dismiss these problems, it's just that we ESPs tend to get overwhelmed by our children's distress and go immediately to the darkest place, even when there is no evidence that a serious problem exists. This results in our responding in ways that are not useful to them (or us!) In this case with Jess, I exuded all sorts of angst about how concerned I was about her negative feelings. I tried to get her to talk to me about what was lurking beneath, which only resulted in her getting more irritable and defensive and pushing me away.

Then I consulted a very wise colleague for help. In so many words, she said that what Jess needed from me was to empathize with how hard mornings can be and that feeling cranky is fine—we all have those moments. I should also be clear that going to school is (what I now call) a "have-to," and then to focus on helping Jess move through the difficult morning to show her I believed she could be in a bad mood *and* manage to go to school. The morning I started to take this approach, I watched Jess walk out the door, despondent, shoulders slumped. My heart was in my stomach. I was an emotional wreck all day expecting a call from the school nurse or that Jess would come home in tears. But at 3:05 p.m., there she was, sauntering down the street, skipping along with a neighborhood friend, all smiles. She had a great day. Lesson learned!

What our kids need is for us to: tune in to and empathize with their experience; tolerate their distress (as hard as that is); set a limit that helps them move forward; and then, when they are regulated, brainstorm what tools might help them cope in the challenging moment.

I need to manage my expectations of my child. Your child is going to have more frequent and intense meltdowns than those less sensitive and intense kids who make their parents look soooo good! It's not your fault. It's the "expectation gap" that causes so much frustration and despair. You expect your child to be able to manage a transition, a disappointment, something unexpected—no matter how much amazing preparation you have done to avoid the meltdown—and they still fall apart.

Here's a powerful and profound example of how managing expectations can lead to more sensitive and effective parenting, shared by a mom of a seven-year-old whose nervous system gets overwhelmed easily. He descends into dysregulation *very* quickly and fiercely when he is not completely in control of a situation. He is demand-avoidant and can be explosive and destructive.

> I was trying so hard to stick to the screen limit of sixty minutes a day for Spencer [seven]. Then, one day I decided to trust what I know about him: he is so sensitive and intense that by the time he gets home after a long day at school, he needs to just completely zone out and decompress. The screen provides that.

So, I started letting him watch (only appropriate content) up to two hours before dinner. And guess what? He is a total delight for the rest of the night—so much more regulated. We have lots of warm conversations and connections. Before, it was just one explosion and battle after another—with maybe ten total minutes of peace. That's when I realized that this was good parenting, not "permissive" parenting, and that it wasn't ruining my child to let him have more screen time than "experts" recommend. They don't know my child and family or what we need. We have so much less stress and so much more bonding. That's a net positive.

This mom shared her epiphany about screen time after announcing that she had made a major mindshift. Previously, she had been thinking, "What's wrong with you? Why can't you just come home from school, happily hang up your backpack, wash your hands, have a snack, regale me with all the fun you had at school today, and then just play, instead of falling apart the second you walk in the door, dropping all your stuff on the floor, yelling at me for having the wrong kind of graham crackers, and then being in a rage the rest of the day?" Then she made this shift: "It's amazing that you can go to school all day, follow a million rules, make transition after transition, sit and listen for long periods, and share and take turns with so many other kids. I am in total awe of you." Recalibrating her expectations led to her taking a step back and reassessing some of her parenting decisions, like this one on screen time.

That's why it's not helpful to compare your child to other kids who are more regulated and adaptable. This is a destructive rabbit hole that I hope you will not go down for your own mental health . . . and your child's!

I need to manage my expectations of myself. It's critically important to keep in mind that "gentle" parenting is not some prescribed, one-size-fits-all approach. Being gentle with a big reactor requires a whole different set of tools and heroic self-control. You are not always going to be able to calm your child or to remain calm yourself. It's unrealistic to expect that somehow you will have the Herculean ability to stay cool and loving in the face of those "slaughterhouse screams" (as one dad put it), or when your child is spewing venom to the tune of, "You are a bad, mean mommy monster and I'm going to throw you in the trash," even when you know they don't mean it. As one mom noted about her child: "Once she's triggered, there's no calming her. We have to let her reach her apex and then peter out."

Staying warmly connected may mean taking your own break from your child in order to help yourself calm and avoid reactivity. Connection and co-regulation may not be giving your child a bear hug or guiding your child to take deep breaths (because they are rejecting any and all calming tools). It may be sitting on the other side of the door and repeating a loving mantra to keep you and your child safe when they are spiraling out of control and being destructive. This lets your child know that you can tolerate their distress and that they are not alone.

I find that once parents manage their expectations and give themselves some grace, they are better able to be the rock their big reactors need them to be. They accept that they will need breaks from their children to prevent reactivity and to remain a calm and loving presence; and that these breaks, done lovingly, are helpful, not harmful. (See the appendix for a resource on how to set up and implement safe space breaks.)

My child doesn't need me to fix their problems and make it all better. Parents of big reactors often find themselves jumping in to fix whatever problem their child is struggling with, especially when they are acting as if it's a five-alarm fire. They worry that their child's level of distress must be harmful to them and, thus, must be alleviated, stat. They fear that struggling will erode their child's sense of self-confidence and lead to low self-esteem.

When our child's distress becomes our distress, we also need relief. This results in parent-to-the-rescue, unintentionally sending the message that we don't think our child is capable of mastering the challenges they face; that only we can solve their problems. This is how the expectation that we should be able to prevent all pain and find all fixes evolves over time.

Instead, think of yourself as your child's problem-solving partner. Let them know that you have confidence in their ability to learn to solve the challenges they encounter, that they can do hard things. You will always help them think it through and help them come up with solutions. But you won't solve their problems for them because that is their job.

There is no true gentle parenting without limits. Limits are loving, even when your child doesn't like them and melts down in the face of them. In the absence of limits, children tend to spiral out of control, redouble their demands, and draw you into painful power struggles. You end up walking on eggshells around them. These are all dynamics that increase stress, make parents feel angry and resentful, and create obstacles to being the loving, empathetic parent your child needs you to be and that you want to be. Limits show children you believe in them and that they can learn to handle it when they don't get what they want when they want it. This builds confidence, cooperation, and peace in families.

My job is to give my child what they need, which is not necessarily what they want. Kids are bottomless pits. It's in their DNA to want more of everything. No amount of sweets, screen time, cuddle time, or playground time will feel like enough. They may want endless books at bedtime, but that delays sleep and results in protracted negotiations (a.k.a. power struggles) that cause significant stress for you and your child. Your child may want you to dress them at an age when they are perfectly capable of doing it themselves. Doing it for them impedes the development of important skills and erodes their sense of independence and self-confidence.

That's where limits come in and why they are loving, even when your child doesn't make you feel like you are being loving. They accuse you of starving them when you won't be a short-order cook; they proclaim that you love their sibling more when you tell them they need to share the coveted truck with their brother. A five-year-old cries, "Mama, you're breaking my heart," when her mom puts a limit on cuddle time (which is already fifteen minutes) before lights-out.

What your big reactor needs is for you to validate their desires and stick to the limit versus trying to get them to accept or agree that they should be satisfied with what they are getting: "I know, it will never feel like enough cuddle time (books, screen time, treats). I love it too. But it's time for lights-out. I can't wait to see you in the morning and give you a big hug."

Less is almost always more. Harry (seven) is a very big reactor. His parents shared that after a lot of hard work on managing their own emotions and being less reactive to him when he is having a difficult moment, Harry is now much better able to soothe himself. He will even voluntarily go into his room to take a break. They asked me if it was okay to let him do this. They have heard so much about the importance of tuning in to and acknowledging children's feelings. They worry Harry won't know that they are there for him—that they care about his emotions—and wonder if they should follow him and get him to talk.

Here is a child who has learned an amazing skill—to regulate himself in such a healthy and positive way. He is clearly letting his parents know that this is what he needs. There will be opportunities to talk about feelings and to show that they see and understand him. But pursuing him in this moment would likely be experienced as intrusive—not respecting his boundaries.

Yes, I am a mental health professional who has dedicated more than three decades to supporting children's social and emotional well-being. And yes, I believe that tuning in to and validating feelings is critically important for children's mental health and for healthy parent–child relationships. But what I see happening now is that parents have been led to believe (largely via popular Instagram accounts) that leaning deep into feelings is *always* what kids need; that not doing so sends the message that you don't care about your child's feelings and are abandoning them in their moment of distress. This notion has had a very detrimental effect on many of the families I work with. Instead of following their children's lead (true "gentle" parenting), they are being intrusive and often inadvertently escalating their children's dysregulation, not supporting their emotional regulation.

I see this in the hours of audio/video of meltdown moments I get each week from families that show a parent (often the ESP) making repeated supportive statements along the lines of, "This is a tough moment. I'm here with you," "This is so tricky. I see you're so sad. I am sorry you are so unhappy," to show empathy and acceptance of their child's emotions. They ask about the child's feelings—why they are sad or mad.

What I also observe is that, in the heat of the moment, this approach backfires. The more parents repeat supportive phrases when their child is melting down, the more dysregulated the child gets. Kids are shouting: "Stop talking!" or "Go away, mommy, you are not being a kind friend!" or, "I am not angry!" Their brains are flooded with cortisol (a stress hormone), and they cannot think clearly. It causes more, not less, stress and dysregulation.

What kids need when it comes to exploring emotions is highly dependent on context and timing. It's not helpful when it's intrusive—your child *wants* space—such as the example above. It's also not helpful when children are in a high-arousal, agitated state. When children are in "red zone," repeating an empathic statement doesn't make you more empathetic. They are not able to absorb the meaning and intention of your supportive words. Too much language is overwhelming to their brains. *More is not better in these moments.*

For the vast majority of the families I see each year, the root cause of the challenge for which they are seeking consultation is an absence of limits and the power struggles that flourish in this void. That is what is making everyone miserable—parents and children—and is resulting in less, not more, emotional regulation (for kids and parents!). Often, a key obstacle to implementing loving and critically important limits is parents getting caught up in and worried about their child's feelings. There is a way to be empathetic—to tune in to and validate your child's emotions—*and* help them adapt to and cope with everyday tasks and expectations. That is the needle that you will see being thread through the stories in this book.

CASES

Sloane Struggling with Separations

The Presenting Problem

Sloane (six) is an awesome kid. She is super bright, funny, and charismatic. She is also very intense. Her parents, Maria and James, describe her as living life at the extremes. When Sloane is happy, she is elated. When things aren't going her way, or she's facing something unexpected, she can have epic meltdowns. Of note is that Sloane also has a strong preference for Maria. She wants mom to do everything with her, a dynamic Maria and James have adapted to, even though they know it's not healthy.

Maria and James are motivated to seek my help because of an uptick in some challenging behaviors. It all started when Maria had a five-day business trip. They had read about how important it was to prepare children for absences, especially from a parent the child is most strongly attached to. Accordingly, they made a book with lots of photos of Maria and Sloane together; they talked about it for weeks in advance so Sloane would know what to expect; and they planned to video chat several times a day. During the period before Maria left, Sloane started to get very irritable and dysregulated. There was an uptick in tantrums and demanding behavior. She was hyper-focused on mom leaving, asking every day if she was going to be home when Sloane returned from school. Despite the advance notice and a lot of communication with Maria while she was away, Sloane had a very hard time with Maria's absence. She insisted on calling mom almost constantly. This resulted in a lot of battles with James, especially when he was trying to get Sloane through an important routine—getting ready for school or bed. The fighting with dad led to an increase in Sloane's overall distress and dysregulation.

Since Maria's return, Sloane has become even more clingy to and demanding of her mom and is totally rejecting James. She insists that Maria does everything with and for her—the whole morning and evening routine—and that Maria not pay any attention to Sloane's two-year-old brother, Alfie. A new wrinkle is that, while previously Sloane was totally fine when Maria dropped her off at extracurricular activities, like gymnastics, she now insists that Maria stay where Sloane can see her throughout the class.

It is noteworthy that none of this is affecting Sloane at school. She is super happy there and has no issues separating from mom or dad at school drop-off. (For an in-depth look at why kids are superstars at school and "terrors" at home, see chapter 8.)

The Analysis

- Being an intense, sensitive child, we expect that Sloane would have a big reaction to her first experience with a long separation from mom.
- We suspect that the approach Maria and James took to prepare Sloane for the last trip backfired because they told her too far

in advance, which caused a lot of anticipatory anxiety. Six-year-olds don't have a firm grasp of time. All Sloane knew was that mom was going to be leaving for a long period of time, which she then hyper-focused on, increasing her anxiety. She had no way of fully comprehending when this separation would take place and what it would feel like. She couldn't benefit from advance notice to imagine and prepare herself for this upcoming change. Young children also don't have the perspective older children and adults have that comes from lots of experience dealing with separations and knowing they can handle and survive them. Thus, telling Sloane about the impending separation weeks ahead of time backfired, increasing her worry.

- The communication plan also backfired because, absent any clear boundaries, Sloane believed she could connect with mom any time of day. All of her focus and energy went into doing just that—badgering dad to call mom. This propelled her into a constant state of agitation. This is one of those situations where what a child wants is not necessarily what she needs; when limits are loving, and more is not better.

- Sloane insisting that Maria stay at all activities is not surprising given her worry about separations from mom. But it's not healthy for Sloane to live with this anxious attachment to her mom. Sloane's ability to separate at school and thrive there is a major strength we want to build on to help her with other separations.

- The parental preference, wanting to "own" Maria, isn't healthy for Sloane or anyone in the family. She shouldn't have the power to effectively shut out James and to prevent Maria from paying attention to and caring for Alfie. Sloane needs to have a strong, loving relationship with both of her parents and not have the power to decide which parent does what.

Addressing the Parental Preference

A child having a "preferred" parent is very common in the families I work with because their kids are fierce and make fierce attachments. Some children develop a strong attachment to the parent who is acting as the primary caregiver—the one who is getting them through daily tasks and routines and who does most of the comforting. It doesn't happen solely in families with a stay-at-home parent but usually occurs when one parent shoulders the bulk of the caregiving responsibility. This is often the parent who is the ESP because they are more focused on sensitive caregiving and may be less firm about limits.

It is also common for a child to favor one parent over the other when there's a new baby in the family. In some cases, the older child starts to rely more heavily on the parent who hasn't given birth, whom they perceive as more available. Other times it's the converse, the child clings to the parent who birthed the new baby. Sometimes the genesis of the preference is unclear. Regardless, it's usually a way for the child to cope with a complex or challenging situation. For Sloane, we hypothesize that the preference for Maria has been amplified by what felt like a very long separation.

Whatever the underlying reason for the preference, when there are two parents, it's important for children's healthy development (and for a healthy marriage/partnership) that kids develop a close, trusting relationship with both parents. It's not healthy for kids to have "anxious" attachments[2] that are characterized by fear of separation or abandonment. Also, children should not have the power to decide which parent can do what—put them to bed, get them breakfast, take them to school. Those are "mommy/daddy" decisions.

The Plan

Maria and James always start by telling Sloane exactly what to expect. If dad is in charge of breakfast, they let Sloane know that if she needs anything, he is her guy. When she demands that mom, who is getting ready for work or taking care of Alfie, prepare her oatmeal, James calmly acknowledges Sloane's desire. He reminds her that he is the helper and when she is ready, he is happy to get her breakfast. He is silly and uses humor to engage her and to signal that he is not distressed about her wanting mom. He is not taking it personally. He acts dumb—like he isn't sure where the raisins are that she likes on her oatmeal. He acts like he can't count correctly: "Let's see, I think I want ten raisins in my oatmeal, one, three, seven . . ." When Sloane demands that mom help her get dressed on a morning when dad is in charge, James responds: "I know you want mommy right now, but daddy is the clothes helper this morning. I am your guy if you want help, let me know."

This is also when the "have-to" and the "two-great choices" can be very helpful. (See the appendix for resources that discuss, in depth, how to use these tools.) Maria and James have explained to Sloane that the "have-to" is that they leave at 8:30 a.m. to be at school on time.

It is a mommy/daddy job to make sure that happens. The great news is that Sloane has two great choices: option one is that she cooperates with putting on the school clothes that she likes; option two is that she chooses not to put school clothes on (or she can't because she is too out of sorts to process the choice) and she goes to school in what she is wearing when they have to leave. In that case, they will put a set of clothes in her backpack. Her teacher said she can change at school whenever she wants. (This is a strategy that has worked for many families whose kids fight getting dressed and tear their clothes off as soon as parents wrangle them on.)

To connect with Sloane's desire to be in charge, they acknowledge that they can't force her to get dressed, nor will they do that. They tell her that *they* choose to put on work clothes when they start their day because they don't feel comfortable working in pajamas. It's her body and she has to make her own decision about this. Taking this approach is what I find most loving and effective with kids who are all about control and will take it wherever they can get it. The more you tell them what to do or try to make them do anything, the more they dig in their heels to assert their autonomy, for example, by tearing off the clothes you have just wrestled them into.

They create lots of opportunities for James to have special time with Sloane. When Sloane says she doesn't want to go with dad to the park, out for ice cream, or on a walk with the dog because she wants to stay home with mom, Maria and James acknowledge her desire and, at the same time, are clear that this is a "have-to." They know that if Sloane perceives it as a choice, that they are counting on her agreement with the plan, she will throw up every retort and obstacle to ensure it doesn't happen. In these situations, it's especially important for Maria to add something like "Daddy is the best! I'm so excited to hear all about your adventure with him when you get back." Seeing that Maria is totally supportive of Sloane's relationship with her dad and that she can tolerate the separation from Sloane is important for her forming a more secure attachment with Maria.

This is hard for both Maria and James to execute. Maria worries Sloane will feel rejected by her. James has to exert a lot of self-control not to blurt out, "Fine—stay with your mom. Why do I care? Who would want to take a kid out for ice cream who doesn't want to go?!" But they know that following through is what Sloane needs from them, so they stay the course.

The Outcome

James uses humor and acts silly in moments when Sloane is rejecting him, which helps a lot. When Sloane insists that Maria is the only one who can cut her sandwich, instead of taking it personally and feeling hurt and defensive, James responds: "Wait a minute . . . do you think daddy doesn't know how to cut a sandwich? Boohoo! I am so good at cutting sandwiches! Want to see?" Sometimes, this "gamifying" works. It breaks the tension and Sloan says it's okay, he can cut her sandwich. When humor or being playful doesn't work, he has a plan B. "I know, you want mommy to do it. I don't blame you, she's great at cutting sandwiches; but daddy is the food-helper now so if you want it cut, let me know." Or "I am happy to show you how to cut it yourself. We can do a sandwich-cutting lesson."

When Sloane refuses to let James help her get dressed and is not ready when it's time to go to school, they follow through with the plan and take her to school in her pajamas. She protests the entire way there, hurling lots of venom about how mean they are. When they get to the parking lot, through her sobs, Sloane asks if she can change into her school clothes before she goes into school. Mom says that sounds like a great idea. Victory. Dressing battles are bygones.

When Sloane refuses to go with James to do an activity and he responds by staying calm and moving her along, she ends up having a blast and they have a wonderful bonding experience. The more experience she has with this new approach, the fewer battles and the more adaptation and joy for this family.

Preparing for the Upcoming Separation

The Plan

Maria and James provide the information in a very matter-of-fact way, without the angsty tone that Maria typically, unintentionally, uses when she shares news that she is worried Sloane will react badly to. HSCs are very reactive to tone. When they sense others' worry, it increases their worry. "Sloane, mommy is going on a work trip on Monday, in two days."

They show Sloane a calendar so she can see exactly what days Maria will be gone. Maria lets her know exactly what to expect: "On Monday, I will be here in the morning to help you get ready and I will drive you to school. Then I will go to the airport to get on a plane to go to Los Angeles. I will be there for three days and will be home on Thursday by the time you get home from school." (Some families go all out and tape photos of the location where the absent parent will be onto the calendar to show the days they'll be away.) It also can be helpful to make it fun by going onto the internet and exploring photos and information about where the parent is going.

They introduce the idea of the "worry brain" versus the "thinking brain." James and Maria explain that there are different parts of our brains. They start with the memory part as most kids can easily relate to it—that it's the part of the brain that helps us remember things. Maria and James make it fun and brainstorm with Sloane all the things her memory brain has already remembered.

Then they explain that we also have a "worry" part of our brain that makes us think something will go wrong, or that we are not okay and safe. And then there is the "thinking" part of our brain that helps our "worry brain" know whether there is really something we need to worry about. It reminds us of past experiences when we overcame fears. They recall with Sloane times when she was afraid or worried but it turned out fine—like when she feared that mom might not come back from that first business trip but now knows that mommy always comes back. Sloane chimes in that she was afraid of swim class but then her thinking brain helped her know that her floaties made the water safe and she had a blast. They also use this as an opportunity to remind Sloane that her "thinking brain" knows she is okay at night on her own in her bed because she slept independently for a very long time before she started sleeping in their bed.

Helping kids look at their brains objectively in this way—that it's something they can think about and control—can ease a lot of anxiety. You will see how this tool works in many other cases shared in this book.

They tell Sloane how they will keep in touch with mommy when she is away. Every day Maria will send a video to Sloane and Alfie to tell them all about her trip and how much she loves them. Daddy will help Sloane and Alfie make a video to send to mommy each day. We came up with this plan based on lessons learned from the last trip. The lack of boundaries totally backfired. They consider including a video call each day, but based on past experience, they are worried that this might also be overwhelming and unhelpful. These calls usually end up with both kids squabbling, fighting for control of the screen, and in tears, turning what is meant to be a time for connection into chaos.

The Outcome

As expected, Sloane initially gets very upset at the thought of mom leaving. Maria and James fully validate those emotions and how big they feel. They avoid jumping in to try to make it all better by assuring Sloane about how much fun they are going to have while mommy is away or how quickly she'll be back. As is true for many big reactors, the more you try to minimize or talk them out of their feelings, the more fiercely they up the ante and double down to be heard.

Also as expected, Sloane begs and demands to communicate with Maria throughout the day, exclaiming that she must talk to mommy "right now! I have something very important to tell her!" This is very difficult for James; it feels mean not to allow Sloane to do this. It takes a lot of his own self-regulation and reminding himself that, while this is what Sloane wants, it's not what she needs. Accordingly, James acknowledges Sloane's desire to talk to mom but holds the limit and tolerates her upset. When she proclaims that she will not be making a video for mommy because he is being mean, James responds that it's her choice. She should let him know if she changes her mind. Once Sloane sees that dad is not changing the plan, and that Alfie is participating in the video-making, she decides to join in. Initially she harrumphs and shouts into the camera that she is very, very mad at daddy for not letting her talk to mommy whenever she wants. When James doesn't react, and lets her share whatever she likes, she softens and sends a loving message to Maria, recounting a very detailed summary of her day.

Sloane is tickled and over the moon when she sees Maria's video response. In subsequent days, Sloane is much calmer and stops badgering James for constant contact with mom.

Dealing with Separations at Activities

The Plan

Maria and James decide to start with gymnastics since that is the activity Sloane enjoys most. They will start with James taking her since she has an easier time separating from him. When Maria takes Sloane to class, she will leave for the entire time. We considered doing it more incrementally, which works for some kids. That plan entails the parent leaving for increasingly longer stretches each consecutive week until the parent leaves for the entire time. Our concern is that if Sloane knows that at some point mom will return, she will focus all of her attention on waiting for mom to come back and not focus on adapting and joining the class. Many teachers/coaches report that kids often do much better when parents are not present. This is likely because kids are so tuned in to their parents' expectations of them, which can feel like pressure, especially for HSCs who tend to be more self-conscious and process praise as evaluation, which, in fact, it is.

Before they execute the intervention, Maria communicates with the teacher to engage her support. She describes the plan to be sure the teacher is comfortable with it. Maria explains that what is most likely to help Sloane is that, after she leaves, the teacher validates how hard it is to say goodbye to mommy; that she totally understands—lots of kids feel that way—and then to offer her a job, for example, to help spread out the parachute or to move some mats. This focuses Sloane's attention on something productive and positive. And Sloane loves jobs. If that works to help her cope and adapt, great. If not, the teacher should let Sloane know that if she needs some space before she's ready to join (i.e., if she is crying and not able to engage) that is totally fine. She can set Sloane up in an area where she is safe and can observe. They can't wait for her to join when she's ready. This approach—showing empathy and then providing space, not persistently cajoling, coaxing, or cheerleading the child to move on and participate—is what helps children calm and move forward more quickly.

The Outcome

When James does drop-off, Sloane seems a little hesitant but adapts fairly quickly. When Maria resumes taking Sloane to class, she clearly explains what to expect: that she will walk Sloane into class, they will do a special "goodbye" ritual, and then mom will go to do mommy tasks while Sloane is in class. She will be back five minutes before class is over so she can watch Sloane do the closing activity. She will bring her a special snack to fill her belly after doing so much good exercise for her body. Still, Sloane is very clingy. She insists and begs for mom to stay or "I will not do anything the whole time!" Maria stays steady, calm, and loving. She tells Sloane that what she does in class is totally up to her. She is in charge of her body. In an upbeat tone, Maria tells Sloane she can't wait to see her when she returns to watch the final activity. At that point, the teacher approaches and guides Sloane away from Maria, who leaves. Naturally, Maria is sick to her stomach and has a horrible hour sitting right outside the building, racked with anxiety about what is going on in the gym.

Once Maria leaves, the teacher shows compassion to Sloane, acknowledging that it's hard to get used to moms or dads not being in class. But Sloane will see that just like she had a great time in class after her dad dropped her off, she has confidence Sloane can also have fun when mommy does the drop-off. She then tells Sloane that she needs a helper to count all the kids as they come into the class and to shout, "All here!" when all ten participants are present. Sloane is still crying hard and doesn't respond. The teacher tells her that she'll give her a minute and will check back with her. In the meantime, she gives Sloane some balls to throw in the pit if she wants. Sloane immediately starts doing just that and begins to calm. The teacher then approaches and asks if she is ready to count the kids, which Sloane does. She brightens. The teacher then begins the class. Sloane is still very teary and keeps looking toward the door. She participates on and off throughout the class. When she sees her mom at the window right as they are lining up to do their final activity/performance, she breaks into a huge smile, starts furiously waving, and with a lot of bravado takes her turn at climbing the foam blocks, jumping off and somersaulting to the end of the mats. Maria is astonished and thrilled. They have a wonderful reunion.

It's a little bit like Groundhog Day for future drop-offs. This is confusing and upsetting to Maria. Now that Sloane sees that she is totally fine at class without her, why would she revert back to worry and distress every time mom leaves? I see this phenomenon quite frequently. It's likely to do with the fact that transitions are often difficult for big reactors. The feelings take over and flood their brains, making it hard for them to access their "thinking brains" that remind them that they have been here before and will be fine. But with time and patience, the needle often moves.

All told, this new approach that Maria and James take makes a significant difference for Sloane and the entire family. Sloane is getting better at managing her big feelings and adapting when things don't go exactly as she wants. She and James are building a closer relationship, and she has a less anxious attachment to Maria.

Leo and the Library

The Presenting Problem

Leo is a very spirited, fierce, and feisty three-year-old. He is highly active and intense. He has big reactions to seemingly everything, according to his mom, Molly. When Leo is happy, he is overflowing with positive energy and excitement. When he's unhappy, because he's not getting something he wants, he can get out of control and be very difficult to contain. Molly wants to be a "gentle" parent and encourage Leo's curiosity and passion for life, but she is struggling. She finds herself walking on eggshells with Leo. She gives in on important limits to avoid major meltdowns. They are too exhausting.

One situation she dreads these days are their visits to the library—one of Leo's favorite activities. It's right across the street from his bus stop. They have a ritual of going every afternoon after she picks him up from school. But it goes off the rails every time. Leo ultimately catapults into overarousal and starts running around like a whirling dervish—tossing books and bumping into other kids. It turns into a tense, physical struggle to get him contained and out of the library. An activity that is intended to be a joyful, shared experience ends with everyone miserable.

The Analysis

As we process this scenario, Molly recognizes that, while going to the library may be what Leo wants, and seems like a great idea theoretically—after all, it's the library!—in reality, after a long day at preschool, it is not what he needs. Leo is on overdrive and needs less, not more, stimulation. It's Molly's job to implement a plan that is supportive to Leo, even if he doesn't like it.

At the same time, Molly is terrified about how Leo will react to a change of plans. She is worried about her ability to follow through. He can get so out of control that she's not sure she can handle it. She is pretty certain—if history is any guide—that when Leo realizes they are not going to the library after school, he is likely to have a major meltdown. She needs a clear plan to keep herself from reacting so she can be the rock Leo needs to weather the depths of his disappointment.

The Plan

We think about the best time to tell Leo about this change in routine. Molly and I agree that too much advance notice might cause Leo a lot of anticipatory anxiety and not be helpful. He will likely ruminate on and badger her about it. At the same time, she doesn't want to blindside him and make this change without warning. Telling him at bedtime the night before is risky, as it is likely to catapult him into distress and dysregulation at a time when his body and mind need to calm down. So, Molly decides to tell him right after dinner the night before she's going to implement the new plan. This way the news won't disrupt dinner and will allow some time before bed to help him calm and connect.

Molly develops a plan to ensure safety and that helps her remain calm through this new transition. Molly knows she may need help getting Leo from the bus to the car given his physicality. Before she implements the plan, she talks to the aide on the bus, Jillian, to enlist her assistance. Molly also anticipates that Leo may throw objects at her once he's in his car seat, so she is prepared to take off his shoes and to remove any toys that are within his reach. She also moves his car seat to the middle where he can't kick the back of her seat. She secures a fidget and a chewable toy to the car seat so he has some safe, soothing tools he can access.

The Outcome

Leo immediately launches his protest upon receiving the news that they won't be going to the library after school. Molly stays calm and acknowledges his upset; she knows how disappointing this is because he loves the library so much and wants to go every day. She resists trying to talk him out of or minimize his feelings. She explains it's a mommy decision and that she doesn't expect him to like or agree with it.

Molly then tries to change his focus by counting how many balls of anger he feels. This is a tool she has used in the past to help Leo manage his big feelings. She asks if he's feeling five or ten balls. He shouts, "I'm feeling a bazillion balls." He continues to shout what a mean mommy Molly is and adds that he is the boss and it's his decision to keep going to the library every day, "And that is that!" Molly doesn't react or start defending herself and her decision. She quietly acknowledges his distress one more time and then tells Leo that she is going to start building a garage for his cars and that she would love a helper when he is ready. As tempting as it is, Molly (like many parents I work with) has found that in the heat of the moment, the more she keeps validating Leo and talking about the incident, the more agitated he becomes. It leads to less, not more, regulation. Once Leo sees that Molly is not going to change her mind, and that she is not distressed by his meltdown, he calms and engages in play with her. He announces he is now just "one hundred balls of angry!"

While they get through the evening, Molly knows that this doesn't mean Leo is going to accept the new plan once it's actually implemented. Indeed, when the bus arrives and Molly guides Leo to the car instead of going across the street to the library, Leo goes ballistic. She has to enlist Jillian's help to safely move him from the bus to the car. Molly whispers to Leo that she knows this is really hard. (Whispering is often calming to both parents and kids in charged moments.) Then she remains a quiet and as-calm-as-possible presence so, together with Jillian, Leo can be secured in his car seat. He is still flailing and hysterical. She sees that Leo is going for his shoes, so she takes those off. She then buckles herself in, puts Leo's favorite music on, and hums along as he continues to rage.

When they arrive home, Leo is still quite dysregulated and screaming about how he needs to go the library. Molly brings him into his room to create a boundary instead of giving him free rein to be destructive in the house. She tells him that she is going to set up their own library and that when he's ready, she'd love him to join.

She chooses one of Leo's favorite books, organizes a bunch of his stuffed animals in a circle, and starts animatedly reading. Leo continues to insist that Molly take him back to the "real" library and starts to hit her. She responds, "Do you need something to hit?" and gives him a pillow. In this way, she sets the limit—that he can't hit her—with her actions instead of triggering him by making it a correction and telling him, "No."

When Leo keeps swiping at her, she tells him she is going to take a mommy moment because she can't let him use his body in unsafe ways. At that point, she leaves, closes the door, and sits on the other side. She hums so he knows she's right there. She ignores Leo's banging on the door and the venom he is spewing. When she hears a pause, she asks if he is ready to help with the library. He doesn't answer but she can hear he is calming. She reenters and asks if he wants a hug. Leo, still sobbing, says, "No!" Molly responds, "No problem I am always here for hugs when you want one," then turns to the stuffed animals and says, "Let's see what happens in this book!" and continues reading. She pauses to ask the animals some questions and answers for them, using lots of humor. She can see Leo is intrigued by this, but resists asking him to join as she knows this may send him back into defensive mode. She picks up one of the animals and has them whisper something in her ear. She says aloud, "Oh, you don't want me to be the librarian in this room, you want Leo to be the librarian? Hmm, I don't know if Leo wants to do that." Leo responds, "Yes I do!" as mom hands him the book and he takes over. Molly has now completely redefined what it means to be a "gentle" parent to Leo.

SHORT STORIES

The following are stories from the trenches that illustrate other common situations where parents of big reactors find themselves.

When Always Trying to Make Your Child Happy Makes Them (and You!) Unhappy

Elizabeth is a single mom by choice. She had yearned for a child for a very long time and had to go through many procedures to have Mireille (five), the HSC featured in the introduction to this chapter. Elizabeth had spent a lot of time fantasizing about the close bond they would have—being on their own, together—and how happy she would make her child. But now Elizabeth finds herself totally exhausted. She feels suffocated by Mireille, whose needs seem to be endless. "If I try to gather a moment of space to regulate myself, which sometimes I need to do to avoid becoming punitive or yelling, it intensifies her distress. She will follow me and come into my physical space. I can feel how desperate she is for my comfort, which I'm absolutely willing to give her, just once I've calmed myself down." Mireille also ruminates. When Elizabeth says they can't go to the playground because it's raining, Mireille will whine and mope, talk incessantly about how much she's missing the swings . . . for hours. She will get a tiny scratch and nurse and complain about it for the entire day.

Mireille protests every limit Elizabeth tries to set, such as no screens during mealtimes and no snacking all day. Elizabeth finds herself often caving on these limits even though she knows this isn't good for Mireille. They're late to school every day, which is becoming a problem. The teacher reports that Mireille is calmer and more engaged when she arrives on time. Joining the class late is dysregulating. She's out of sorts on those days.

Mireille's meltdowns are so epic that Elizabeth worries she's too fragile to tolerate not getting what she wants. She's afraid that, in these moments, Mireille's anger will taint the strong, connected relationship she's trying to build with her—her number one priority. Further, Elizabeth can't tolerate seeing Mireille in distress as she (mistakenly) equates it with being unhappy. She focuses all her energy on rescuing Mireille from any discomfort. She hopes that constantly filling Mireille's cup will make her feel safe, secure, and loved, and to be a happy and content child.

By the time Elizabeth comes to see me, she's beginning to see that this approach isn't making Mireille more content. In fact, she's becoming more demanding and the stress in their relationship is growing—the exact opposite of the connection she's trying to forge with Mireille. That's how she knew it was time to seek help. Through our work, Elizabeth gains the following insights:

- Mireille is actually a very competent child who is quite resilient. At school and with other adults, she is able to manage disappointment and frustration and regulate her big emotions.
- This demand for constant connection may be what Mireille wants, but this kind of unhealthy attachment is not what she needs. It's also not healthy for Elizabeth to feel suffocated by Mireille—to have no personal space, to feel like Mireille is trying to control her, and that she's feeling *at* Elizabeth. This is not enabling her to be the mom she wants to be for Mireille.

- Mireille may want to be in charge, but that's also something that's not good for her or what she needs. This dynamic has resulted in unhealthy outcomes for Mireille, like getting to school late, too much screen time, and too many sweets. She and Mireille are also locked in protracted power struggles that cause Elizabeth great despair and worry.

- The lack of limits is what is causing so much stress in the family and is the biggest obstacle to solidifying the close, trusting relationship Elizabeth so badly wants with Mireille.

With this change in mindset, Elizabeth makes the following changes:

Creating personal boundaries. Elizabeth validates and offers comfort when Mireille is distressed. If this doesn't help and Mireille escalates into raging at her or getting physical, Elizabeth helps both of them take safe-space breaks. When Mireille continues to complain about a minor booboo or incident, Elizabeth doesn't try to convince her that it's not a big deal as that usually results in Mireille upping the ante to show just how serious it is. Instead, Elizabeth acknowledges that Mireille experiences things deeply and that it feels uncomfortable when something unexpected happens to her body. Then she offers to be detectives together to figure out what kind of care she needs. Is it something she can take care of herself, like massaging where she banged her leg to make the owie go away? Something she needs help with, like getting a Band-Aid? Or something that requires a doctor's help? She helps Mireille make a kit with all the things she can use to make it feel better: a few Band-Aids, a compress, some cream. In taking this approach, Elizabeth is empowering Mireille to take care of herself (when there is really nothing wrong). If it requires intervention, of course Elizabeth provides or accesses it.

Removing screens at mealtime. Elizabeth follows through on locking the tablet up during mealtime and tolerating Mireille's upset. When Mireille threatens not to eat if she doesn't get the screen, Elizabeth responds that mommy's job is to offer lots of growing foods; it's Mireille's job to decide how much her belly needs and what she eats. That is something only Mireille can decide and control. She also starts a ritual of telling Mireille a story about her childhood at each meal, which Mireille loves. Not getting into a power struggle and offering positive ways to connect results in fewer meltdowns about screens at mealtime and Mireille eating a full, healthy meal. (See the appendix for a resource on solving mealtime struggles.)

Setting limits on sweets. Elizabeth tells Mireille that it's a mommy job to make sure her body grows healthy and strong. That means she can't let Mireille eat sweet treats whenever she wants. The new plan is that Mireille will be able to choose a snack twice a day—after lunch and after dinner. Elizabeth knows how hard it is to resist treats so she will be a helper by putting a lock on tne cabinet. She understands that Mireille may not like this rule, and she doesn't expect her to. Why would she be happy to not be able to go into the cabinet and get treats whenever she wants? Naturally, Mireille protests and kicks and pulls at the cabinet door. Since this is not actually harming Mireille or the door, Elizabeth doesn't correct her—as that is sure to lead to further dysregulation. Being calm and consistent with this new plan results in a major reduction in battles over sweets.

Establishing a morning routine. Together, Elizabeth and Mireille create a visual schedule, pick out clothes the night before, and design their menu for breakfast. In the morning, if Mireille is having a hard time getting through the tasks, despite all the great preparation the night before, Elizabeth knows how to move her along without engaging in power struggles. If Mireille doesn't cooperate with dressing, despite lots of "gamifying," Elizabeth gets comfortable taking her to school in her pajamas, using the same approach described with Sloane: "We are leaving for school in five minutes (shown on a visual timer). That is the 'have-to.' You have two great choices: you can cooperate with getting dressed and go to school in the clothes you have chosen; or you are choosing to go in your pajamas. That's totally up to you." Implementing this plan just one time ends dressing battles in the mornings. In fact, on day one, Mireille asks to change as soon as they start to leave the driveway.

All told, by getting comfortable with establishing healthy space between them and being a loving limit setter, Elizabeth has dramatically changed their relationship. There are far fewer battles and negotiations that were so exhausting to both Elizabeth and Mireille. Mireille has also become significantly less demanding. Elizabeth is feeling much more loving toward Mireille and better about herself, seeing that she is raising an amazing, strong, and resilient child. Elizabeth also has a lot more energy to play and connect with Mireille. They now have the relationship she had always dreamed of. Getting there just looked a lot different than she had imagined and that she ever thought she had the wherewithal to make happen.

When Going Deep into Feelings Is Not Helpful

Mark and Lacey are getting reports from the teacher that their six-year-old son, Liam, seems very lethargic and irritable. They are worried about this but are at a loss as to how to get him to bed at an appropriate time. The routine keeps getting longer and longer. When they try to say goodnight, Liam says he has more feelings to share. When they ask about these feelings, he seems flustered and often goes off on some totally unrelated tangent.

I often hear about this phenomenon from parents. It's likely because kids today know we are so concerned about their feelings that we will stop everything to explore them. These clever kids have figured out that if they tell their parents they are having big feelings, they will get more attention, extend bedtime, get out of doing a task or activity, be late for school, or divert their parents from setting an important limit. They are not being "manipulative"; it's only natural for a child to want more time with the people they love and to do anything they can to keep that going. Their feelings are valid. The problem is when parents worry that these feelings are somehow harmful to their child and that they need to be processed and worked through immediately. In this case, Mark and Lacey fear Liam will feel rejected if they don't stay with him when he's wanting more time for connection—that it will erode their positive connection with him. But that results in Liam often not falling asleep until after 10:00 p.m. They have to wake him up to go to school and he is very cranky. Mornings are miserable. Mark and Lacey know this pattern is very unhealthy and that it's having a detrimental impact on Liam. This insight empowers them to work on tolerating his understandable disappointment when it's time to say goodnight.

They are ultimately able to set the loving limits at bedtime that ensure Liam gets the sleep he needs . . . and they have the evening *they* need. (See the appendix for a resource on how to solve sleep challenges.)

The take-home: going deep into feelings is not helpful when an important transition needs to be made, such as getting your child to bed at an appropriate hour or getting them to school on time (and you to work on time!). Asking lots of questions about why they are having a hard time and offering up myriad calming strategies or solutions is rarely helpful when it's time to make an important transition. It sounds good in theory, but in practice it often further overwhelms and dysregulates children. What kids need—what connection and respect looks like in these moments—is parents helping them adapt by moving them along and getting them unstuck. They need parents to validate that they're having a difficult time and then help them through it: "Going from home to school feels hard some days. I will be your helper" as you get them as calmly as you can into the car to move them along. Getting stuck with them—trying to process feelings when they are in this dysregulated state—often results in escalation, not calm resolution. The time to go deeper into feelings is when your child is calm, regulated, and able to process and reflect on their emotions. This might be on a car ride or when you are cuddling at bedtime. Trying to do this in the heat of the moment often backfires.

PARENTAL SELF-REGULATION

By the time parents come to see me they have had enough experience seeing that their own big reactions almost always result in more power struggles and more dysregulation—the opposite of what they are trying to nurture in their kids and in their relationship. They know they need to break this cycle, but how?

It starts with developing their own self-control. None of the course corrections and victories described in this book would have been possible without all of these parents doing a heroic job of managing their own strong feelings so that they could be responsive, instead of reactive, in the heat of the moment.

Because of how difficult that is, I developed a concrete tool and approach that helps parents pause before reacting. I call it the *mommy/daddy moment*, which entails these steps:

1. **Matter-of-factly name the problem at hand.** "I have asked you to put your toys away. I see you are having a hard time following that direction."

2. **Tell your child you are going to take a mommy/daddy/parent moment** to buy you time to think about how to solve the problem: "I am going to take a mommy moment to get myself calm so I can figure out how we can solve this problem."

3. **Give your child the choices** that you have come up with as a result of thinking through the situation that enable you to remain in control. "You have two great choices: choice one is you put your toys away and we can add five minutes to your screen time later because you did your job and it saved time; choice two is you don't put your toys away, which means I have to do your job. That takes time, so you will have five less minutes of screen time later. You decide what's a better choice

for you." (See the appendix for resources on how to use the "two great choices" approach.)

This process of taking a parental moment can be even more powerful if you have a partner and you do it together. Consider Charlie, who is refusing to turn off his video game when his moms tell him time is up. Sarah says to Beth: "Hmm, mommy, we have asked Charlie to turn off the tablet, but he is having a hard time with that direction. Let's take a mama/mommy moment to think about how we can help Charlie with this problem." The moms then talk it out in front of Charlie in the same respectful, matter-of-fact way described above. They come up with the two great choices: (1) Charlie can hand the tablet over and get his afternoon tablet time; (2) if he chooses not to give it up voluntarily, they will have to take it out of his hands, which they add may feel uncomfortable for everyone but that is what he is choosing, and he won't get his tablet time later in the day. Regardless of the choice Charlie makes, the important limit is implemented—the tablet goes away when screen time is over. This approach provides a very positive, powerful model of parents collaborating to solve a problem. And it gets parents out of the good cop/bad cop roles that often evolve in families.

STORIES FROM THE TRENCHES

Bedtime Battles

Dev and Nurit are having major bedtime challenges with their daughter, Zoara (four). Each night they rotate doing the routine with her, but when it's Dev's turn, Zoara demands that Nurit join them to read. Dev sometimes spends up to twenty minutes trying to get Zoara to accept that it's his night and mom is doing mommy things. But ultimately, he loses it and storms out of the room in frustration. Zoara starts to scream that she didn't get her books and begs for Nurit who goes to Zoara, settles her down, reads to her, and puts her to bed. Dev and Nurit know that this dynamic is unhealthy for everyone, but they feel stuck. Here's how they resolve it using the mommy/daddy moment:

Dev describes exactly what is happening without judgment or anger. "I want to read to you, but you are having a hard time listening."

He employs the mommy/daddy moment. "I am going to take a daddy moment to think about how I can help us solve this problem." Then Dev starts tapping his head and brainstorms aloud to himself, so Zoara is privy to his process: "Hmm, I see that Zoara really wants mommy to read her books. I get that; she loves book time with mommy, which is great. But mommy and I both want to have a chance to read with Zoara so we have decided to take turns reading each night. It's okay if Zoara doesn't agree with our plan; that's a mommy/daddy decision. So, let's see what Zoara's two choices might be. Hmm . . . well, I guess they are, she can choose to listen to the books or she can choose not to listen as I read. That's totally up to her. I can't force her to listen."

During this time Zoara is stopped short in her tracks, totally mesmerized by her dad's musings. Parents who use this strategy report this phenomenon: just witnessing a parent's calm, rational, and respectful thought process results in a shift in the child, from defiance to cooperation. When your focus is on trying to get your child to change their behavior, it launches them into a "fight" mindset. When you stop trying to control them, it shifts their perspective.

Dev presents the "two great choices" to Zoara. "Okay, sweetie, here are your two choices: (1) you can listen to the books, which I would really enjoy because I love sharing books with you; or (2) you can choose not to listen. That's up to you. But it's a daddy book night so I am going to read and then say goodnight. Mommy has said her goodnight, and you will see her in the morning."

Dev doesn't give Zoara any fodder to react to (i.e., demand that she listen and put all his energy into trying to get her to change her behavior). Instead, he moves along with the plan calmly and lovingly. This, together with Nurit not running to the rescue, results in Zoara eventually settling down into dad's lap.

Morning Moodiness

Everett has struggled mightily with his seven-year-old, Austin, who can be very irritable, "rude," and "obnoxious," especially in the mornings. He has tried being playful to get Austin out of his bad mood, but it makes Austin crankier. When Everett shows empathy for how hard it is to wake up in the morning, Austin shouts back, "Stop talking to me!" When Everett tells him he can't talk that way, Austin's go-to retort is, "I can say anything I want!" Everett finds himself getting into inane arguments with Austin, insisting he cannot communicate this way. This never results in any positive changes.

After we meet, Everett shifts from trying to get Austin to change to altering his own approach. One morning Everett is in the kitchen getting breakfast ready. His easier-going daughter (four) enters and happily sits at the table enjoying her breakfast. She is super chatty and delightful. A few minutes later, Austin enters, clearly very cranky.

Everett gives him a warm pat on the shoulder. Austin pulls away and yells at Everett to stop touching him. In the past, Everett would have reacted with hurt and anger, resulting in total escalation. On this day, Everett quietly says: "Hmm, I feel like I'm going into 'red zone' myself. I am going to take a short daddy break to take my deep breaths." When he returns a few minutes later, Austin is calm, sweet, and solicitous.

Without any words, Everett let Austin know that he would not engage with him when he is on the attack. By extricating himself, instead of giving Austin fodder for a fight, Everett created space for Austin to calm and take responsibility for his behavior. Austin may not be ready to say a literal "I'm sorry," but he figuratively did so by showing love and appreciation when Everett returned.

Of course, it doesn't always work out so swimmingly with kids immediately complying, but that's not the point. The purpose of this strategy is to have a plan that enables you to implement the limit whether your child agrees to the plan or not. It can make the difference in whether a situation escalates or resolves. It's a powerful model for self-regulation; that you are getting revved up and are taking a moment to get calm so you can use your thinking brain to move forward in a productive way.

FINAL THOUGHTS

Sensitivity is a strength, not a weakness. HSCs need our support to help them manage their big emotions and reactions that they come by honestly. Then watch them thrive.

3

Inflexibility and Intense Need for Control

Henry threw a huge fit because I picked him up from childcare instead of Grandma who usually gets him at the end of the day.

Chelsea refused to take a bath because I turned on the water when she wanted to do it herself.

Alice insists to be first at everything. She has major fits if her sister orders first in the restaurant or if she isn't first in line to enter school.

If any of these scenarios sound familiar, you are not alone. One of the chief concerns from parents I work with is that their highly sensitive children (HSCs) can be super rigid and controlling. The term "fascist dictator" has been invoked in more consults than I can count. These children have a very hard time being flexible—to adapt when they can't get exactly what they want, when they want it, or when something unexpected happens.

WHY FLEXIBILITY IS SO IMPORTANT

Flexibility is one of the most important assets for functioning well in this world. It's an essential ingredient for adapting to the countless events in life that we can't predict or control. It also helps us work effectively in groups and develop healthy relationships because it enables us to take into consideration the perspectives and needs of others.

Learning to be flexible is a muscle that starts developing very early in life. A two-year-old accepts making a fort with pillows when they can't go to the playground because it's raining. A four-year-old gives up his space at the sand table to a classmate who hasn't had a turn yet. A six-year-old accepts the job of snack helper when they can't be the line-leader. As children grow, this translates into the ability to cooperate on a group project at school or on a sports team and, later, to be a good colleague in the office and a good partner at home.

WHY HSCs HAVE A HARD TIME BEING FLEXIBLE

Go-with-the-flow kids, also known as "dandelions," are more adaptable by nature. They are not as deeply affected by their experiences in the world, so when their parent explains that only the red cup is available, not their favorite blue cup, they can pivot and accept the less desired option. No biggie. (You can see how they make their parents look soooo good.)

Big reactors tend to have a harder time being flexible because of their intense desire for control. They are such deep and constant processors with no "off" button. This means they can get overwhelmed easily by all they are absorbing—making them feel out of control on the inside. To cope, they try to control whatever they can on the outside.

Dictating where people will sit, how loud the music can be, the exact bowl they need for their cereal, the clothes they will and will not wear, or how close the chicken can be to the carrots on their dinner plate—seemingly irrational demands—are all coping mechanisms HSCs use to control their environment.

When things don't go the way they want or expect, it can result in what appears to be outsize, irrational reactions and sometimes major meltdowns. A three-year-old falls apart in a restaurant that doesn't have chicken nuggets shaped like dinosaurs—the only ones she'll eat. A five-year-old gets out of control when he finds his sister in the chair next to mom at dinner and demands she move. A seven-year-old insists her grandfather make a completely new sandwich because he cut it horizontally instead of vertically.

Then there is Nico, who wakes up from a nap in the car in a rage and demands his mom drive back to the spot where he had fallen asleep on the way home from school. The idea that he had not *chosen* to fall asleep and missed all the landmarks he's used to tracking on their drive home triggers him to feel out of control. He wants to undo it to get back to what he knows and expects.

I frequently hear stories like this of children demanding their parents do a reversal in order to replay things exactly as they want and expect, to regain a sense of control; like Stacia (two), who insisted her dad drain all the water from the tub he had filled because *she* wanted to fill it. One mom called this phenomenon "taping the pretzel:" a situation in which you find yourself going to insane lengths to appease your child who has flipped out over something completely irrational, like trying to fix their pretzel that has broken in two, or walking back up the stairs you had already walked down because your child demands to be first.

HSCs who have a low threshold for sensory input—who get overwhelmed easily by loud or sudden noises, clothing textures, people invading their space, or big smells—may have an even harder time being flexible. They are triggered into discomfort by seemingly benign sensory experiences. To protect themselves from unwanted or unexpected sensations, HSCs can become very controlling, which results in inflexibility. Emmy, for example, refuses to use the automatic toilets at the mall because of the sudden, loud sounds they make. She insists they go all the way home so she can go to the bathroom where she is comfortable.

THE TROUBLE WITH TRANSITIONS

HSC's intense need for control can make transitions very difficult because:

- They are zealous about asserting control over their world. This means that whenever there is a demand to follow someone else's agenda, which often entails moving to a task they are not interested in or excited about, there is a natural tendency to resist it.

- HSCs become intensely absorbed in what they are doing. Making a transition requires shifting their energy and attention, which can feel taxing and overwhelming.

- Morning and nighttime routines are associated with separations: going to childcare/school and saying goodnight.

HSCs tend to make fierce attachments that can make separations more difficult.

- HSCs tend to want to stay in their comfort zone, even when the activity they need to move to is one they are familiar with and enjoy. As one mom described: "My four-year-old was very hesitant when I signed her up for gymnastics class. After a few sessions, she started to join in and now she *loves* it. I can't get her out of there when class is over. But every week, when it's time to go back, she fights tooth and nail, insisting she doesn't want to go. It's like Groundhog Day. I just don't get it." The emotional and physical energy it takes to make a transition overrides their memory about how much they love the activity they are going to.

- HSCs are deep processors. When they are expected to transition to a totally new experience, like a new school, new home, or new activity, their wheels are turning, and they wonder: What will happen in this new setting, what will the people be like, will they know how to do whatever skills are required and expected? This phenomenon is addressed in depth in chapter 5 on kids who are cautious and slow to warm up.

Then there is the phenomenon some parents experience in which their child has a really difficult time with the micro, day-to-day transitions, such as having to stop playing to get ready for bed, leaving the house to go to school, or going to a family friend's home for dinner. But they do great and thrive on the big-deal, macro events, such as taking a trip to a new place, moving to a new home, or starting a new school. They are eager for the big changes but sweat the seemingly much smaller stuff.

We can't know exactly why kids do what they do at any given moment. We can't do a PET scan to see what's going on in their brains. But the pattern I see with these kids is that they find macro changes novel and exciting. This puts them in a very positive, energized state and they thrive. The more mundane daily routines or events are not particularly exciting. They feel more stressful, hence the discomfort and resistance.

Helping HSCs learn to be flexible takes time and patience—but it is critically important for healthy functioning in this complex world. While it may seem easier to just take the favored red bowl out of the dishwasher and give it to the child who is demanding it, or to let your child sit next to you at every meal to avoid the meltdowns, it's important not to give in and reinforce your child's rigidity. Helping children learn to be flexible means getting comfortable with their discomfort. They need to go through the experience of not always getting what they want so they can see that they can survive when things don't go exactly the way they expect. The world doesn't adapt to us, we have to adapt to the world.

DEMAND AVOIDANCE

The concept of "demand avoidance" has gone viral in recent years. It describes a knee-jerk, defiant reaction some kids have to any direction to cooperate with a task or to make a transition. It's a common, vexing phenomenon in families with kids who are controlling and inflexible.

This pattern of behavior has been officially termed "pathological demand avoidance" (PDA), but many professionals in the early childhood field, myself included, prefer "pervasive demand avoidance." It's a biological phenomenon and is not purposeful opposition or defiance.[1] The nervous system interprets the demand as a threat to the child's autonomy and triggers a stress response that prepares the body to fight or flee.

While PDA is associated with ASD (autism spectrum disorder), I work with hundreds of families each year and see many kids who are not on the autism spectrum but are prone to demand avoidance because of their intense need to feel in control. When given a seemingly benign direction, such as to start or stop doing something, they process it as others trying to control them. The child experiences this as a threat to their autonomy and their "fight brain"[2] takes over, catapulting them into defiance mode. Resisting the demand is a way to feel in control.

Understanding the root cause is important. At the same time, the reality is that there are many tasks that have to be done to keep children healthy and safe and to run an effective household, especially a busy one with multiple kids: teeth need to be brushed; kids need to be at school, doctor appointments, and activities on time; baths/showers have to be taken; and kids need to stay safely in their rooms at night to get the sleep they need.

You will see in the cases that follow that there are ways to effectively engage the cooperation of kids who are allergic to demands and to help kids be more flexible—to accept and cooperate with the myriad tasks and expectations that make up daily life.

We start with some key parental mindshifts that can help you help your child manage the discomfort of not being in control of everything all the time and develop the flexibility that will help them manage life's frustrations and disappointments.

MINDSHIFTS

My child is not acting like a dictator on purpose. It can be very triggering when your child is in a state of discomfort and responds by ordering you and others around, "You know I hate this kind of chicken nugget! You need to get me the ones I like!" The tone your child takes is mortifying, "obnoxious," and totally unacceptable. Reminding yourself that your child is a great kid having a difficult moment can help. It can put you in a mindset that enables you to be less reactive and more effective in teaching your child the lesson you want to get across.

My child is not a spoiled brat who needs to be toughened up. They are easily triggered into discomfort and need my help to cope. The cause of your child's upset may seem maddeningly minor and irrational. It may make you feel ashamed—like you are raising a spoiled brat. When you see it from your child's perspective and feel compassion for how hard it is for them to manage when something unexpected happens, it enables you to respond in a more supportive and ultimately effective way, which also forges a trusting bond with your child: "I know, you don't like that the banana broke. You want it to be in one piece. I understand. I can't give you a new banana. I can help you find ways to still enjoy this banana. Or you can choose not to eat it. It's up to you."

What my child wants is not necessarily what they need. Your child is going to want you to prevent all discomfort and fix all of their problems, and there's nothing wrong with that. But that's not the way the world works. We all have to deal with unexpected events, frustrations, and disappointments as we journey through life. One of the greatest gifts you can give your child is to help them manage these difficult and inevitable moments. That means you're going to be setting limits that they don't want but need. You won't be running to get your child a new banana or turning around and going all the way back to school so your child can track the route home without falling asleep and missing anything.

I can't control my child; I can control the situation. Big reactors are like heat-seeking missiles when it comes to gaining power. They are dead set on being in charge, which results in pervasive struggles for most families I see. As we reflect on these maddening interactions to get to the root cause, one major insight is that almost every parent is focusing all their attention on trying to control their child—to get them to change their behavior: to agree to stop playing and get ready for bed, to stay in bed after lights-out, or to sit at the dinner table.

As I watch lots of videos and listen to hours of audio of these encounters, what becomes clear is that the more parents try to get their kids to cooperate, the more their kids resist, obfuscate, escalate, or become increasingly provocative to assert their autonomy and show their parents, "You're not the boss of me." All the tactics parents employ to get their big reactors to comply, in fact, puts the outcome in the children's hands and keeps them in charge. Parents use threats, bribes/rewards, nagging, cajoling, and logic ("Don't you want to go to sleep so your body will be big and strong in the morning?"); or gamifying, which sometimes works but often loses its allure for children at some point, not to mention it can be exhausting! Parents are hoping against hope that one of these strategies will result in their children changing their minds and doing the right thing: climbing into the car seat, putting their toys away, and agreeing to sit at the dinner table.

What I observe time after time is children not being swayed by their parents' logic, not accepting the bribe or reward, and not conceding for fear of the threat. For example, in one of many similar situations, the parent threatens, "If you don't stay in your room after lights-out, I'm going to take your lovey away." The child responds by handing the lovey over to her dad as she continues to prance around the house for hours past her bedtime.

Children are very strategic. They quickly figure out that their parents are so eager for them to comply with an expectation/limit/direction, that they engage in "extortion" as one dad framed it. The child will follow a direction or make a good choice only if they receive some reward or special treat for complying. They'll stay in their bed after lights-out if mom reads them five more books. They will sit at the dinner table, but only if they can bring their tablet and watch a show.

But perhaps the most important reason not to go down this rabbit hole of trying to control your child is because . . . you can't control your child. Only they control what they say and do. You can't make them agree to get into a car seat, brush their teeth, stay in bed at night, or cooperate with any limit. *What you do control is the situation* by providing the supportive structure and appropriate boundaries your child needs to follow these important directions. This mindshift will help you focus your attention and actions on what you *can do that is within your power* to help your child follow a direction or limit *that does not depend on your child's cooperation*. (See the appendix for resources on how to parent without power struggles.)

Limits Are Loving and Scaffold Adaptation, Flexibility, and Resilience

Limits create opportunities for children to learn to muscle through challenges and develop strong coping skills. When you set a limit on how much time you will spend trying to get your child's blankets "just right," they ultimately learn to arrange their own blankets and not be dependent on you to do it. When you don't give them a new banana when theirs breaks, they learn to accept and maybe even fix a broken banana by connecting the pieces with peanut butter! When you don't get them dressed when they are at an age when they are fully capable of doing this task independently, they learn to do it themselves and feel awesome about it.

CASES

Nico: It's Never Enough

The Presenting Problem

Chris and Amanda are at their wits' end with their six-year-old, Nico. They feel like he is holding them, and the whole family, hostage. He has to control everything. He can't handle it when something doesn't go the way he wants or expects. If his pretzel breaks, he demands a new one. They bring the snack he chose for the playground, but he changes his mind and demands they go back to the house to get the snack he wants. When he hears mom or dad go downstairs in the morning with his sister, Charlotte (four), he goes nuts and insists they come back up so he can go down first.

Nico is the child referred to earlier in this chapter who fell asleep in the car on the way home from school and fell apart when he woke up and saw they were already in their driveway. He demanded Amanda drive all the way back to the spot where he had fallen asleep (fifteen minutes earlier!).

Nico also does a lot of "equalizing" (or, as Chris calls it, "extortion")—demanding something in exchange for his cooperation. They say it's time to stop playing and get ready for bed. Nico responds that he will do that only if he can have a treat at bedtime. Chris tells Nico he can't have more screen time. Nico says that means dad has to read extra books at bedtime. When they tell him it's time to go to Greek School—not a preferred activity—he says he'll only go if they give him two hours of video games when he gets home to make up for all the time he was at that "boring" school. Even though they don't feel good about this dynamic, Amanda and Chris have been giving in to all Nico's demands because they don't see any other way to get him to do what he needs to do, and because his meltdowns are so unpleasant. They know it's unhealthy for all of them.

Another troubling factor is that Nico constantly accuses them of being bad parents when he doesn't like a limit they are setting: they aren't listening to him; they don't care about his feelings. When they offer a range of foods at dinner, he almost always demands different options and accuses them of wanting him to starve; they only make what *they* like, never what he likes. Chris and Amanda find themselves in endless loops, defending their decisions which of course never satisfies him or results in great cooperation. ("Oh, I see, you're offering me these healthy choices so my body can grow big and strong. Good point. Please pass the spinach.")

Chris and Amanda are miserable and very sad. There is so much more stress than joy in their family life. They also worry about the constant power struggles—it can't be good to be fighting with their child all day—and about the fact that they often give in because they are so worn down. They are very uncomfortable knowing that they are making parenting decisions they don't feel good about in order to avoid Nico's meltdowns.

They are also concerned about Nico absorbing all of their focus and energy, "sucking the oxygen out of our entire family," and the impact this is having on his sister, Charlotte, who is much easier going. She demands and gets much less attention. She is already starting to forgo her own desires to appease Nico. When he insists that she can't play with a toy (that he hasn't shown any interest in for years), she hands it over. She lets him make all the choices, for example, about which TV show to watch. And she always lets him go first—to keep the peace. Chris and Amanda feel stuck and don't know how to turn things around.

The Analysis

Nico is not acting this way on purpose. He is triggered into fight mode when his autonomy is threatened, and he doesn't feel in control. He is trying desperately to avoid the discomfort he experiences at not being in charge and having everything go the way he wants, and it has worked. Chris and Amanda have had a hard time setting the boundaries he needs to learn to manage this discomfort. They now see that giving in to him and getting into protracted battles has been harmful to all of them. They feel ready to start setting limits, to tolerate his distress in order to help him be more flexible, adaptable, and less demanding.

The Plan

We agree that before they tackle specific challenges, they need to repair their relationship with Nico, to move from anger and resentment to empathy and support by taking the following steps:

Chris and Amanda tune in to Nico and validate his personhood. It starts with a heart-to-heart that happens in a quiet moment when Nico is regulated and open to taking in information, not in the heat of the moment. This is a very different approach than Nico is used to. It's not the "there's a new sheriff in town" lecture to discuss his misbehavior that puts him on the defensive and shuts him down, making problem-solving impossible.

Accordingly, at bedtime, when they are cuddling, they tell Nico that they have been thinking about what an amazing human he is. He has an incredible brain and very strong ideas about how he wants things to be. They recount many examples of how this has been great for him. He wants to be first in line at school so he does all his morning tasks on his own very quickly so they can get out the door early. He takes really good care of his toys so that they don't get messed up or lost. When he was dead set on doing all the monkey bars, he didn't give up until he had reached his goal. And then there was the time when his brain was able to be flexible—they had forgotten his swim goggles at home, and he accepted an extra pair they had at the pool. (The alternative of not being able to swim motivated him to adapt.)

They then acknowledge that because Nico's brain has such strong ideas about what he wants, when things don't go the way he expects, it's very hard for him: like when he wants to play another video game but time is up or it's his sister's turn to choose the playground and it's not the one he wants to go to. They show compassion and understanding for how tough these situations can be for him.

They also acknowledge that these things are going to happen: there will be times when Charlotte goes downstairs before him because she wakes up earlier, when he has to stop playing a game because it's time for dinner, when he can't get a toy at the store because they are only buying groceries that day, or when he doesn't like the food choices they are offering at dinner. That's just the way the world works, and it's their job to help him cope with these routine frustrations and disappointments.

They explain how they are going to be his helpers. Chris and Amanda start by sharing their own examples of times when things didn't go the way they wanted, the frustration they felt, and how they had to learn to cope. Chris shares a story of when he had to drop a package off at the post office and he was in a rush. When he arrived, there was a huge line. He panicked and wanted to scream out in frustration. He felt like pushing his way to the front of the line. But he knew that would make other people very uncomfortable and that he would probably have gotten kicked out of the post office and not been able to send the important package. So, he had to take his deep breaths and manage those big feelings so he could wait his turn. They both explain that their parents helped them learn to cope in difficult situations and they are going to help him learn to manage his big feelings, too, because it's their job.

They apologize for engaging in battles with him. "Nico, we also want to apologize. We have not been doing our job. We have been fighting with you, getting frustrated, and raising our voices. We are going to work hard not to do that anymore." When you act in ways that are not loving or kind, apologizing is a gift to you and your child. This kind of repair builds a strong, trusting relationship. You are also serving as a very powerful role model for reflecting on and taking responsibility for your actions—exactly the skills you are trying to teach your child. It also opens kids up and makes it much less likely they will get defensive and shut down the conversation.

Further, taking the blame, telling your child that you've made a mistake, can be very effective; it defies their expectation that this talk is going to involve correcting them for misbehavior, which puts kids on the defensive and shuts them down. Instead, it makes it more likely children will be open and absorb the important information you want to share.

They *don't* apologize when they haven't done anything wrong. For example, when Chris calmly tells Nico it's time to clean up to get ready to go to camp and Nico scolds, "It's not appropriate to interrupt someone when they are building"; when Amanda tries to hold a limit on cuddle time (which is already a solid fifteen minutes) and Nico declares, "You're a mean mommy. You don't care about my feelings"; and when they arrive at the park to find it closed for repairs, Nico accuses, "You lied! You said we could go to the playground today."

These are very tough moments, especially for Amanda who is an emotional support parent (ESP). When our kids accuse us of not loving them or treating them unkindly or unfairly, we worry that we have done something wrong and so we apologize, "I am so sorry! I didn't mean to interrupt you." Or we feel the need to set the record straight because their accusation is so untrue and we get defensive, "Of course I care about your feelings. You know how much I always want to hear what you have to say," and then we give in on the limit to prove our love.

The problem with apologizing or getting defensive in situations when you have *not done anything wrong*—for example, when your child accuses you of being mean for setting a limit they don't like or when something happens unexpectedly that causes disappointment—is that it sends an unhelpful message that it's your fault when you are setting an important limit, or that it's your fault when something upsetting happens. The goal is to help kids ultimately understand and experience that limits are loving, not harmful, and that life involves learning to accept when things don't happen the way they want.

Further, if these accusations end up having the power to derail you from setting limits that your child doesn't like, they gain traction and their power is reinforced. This makes the whole limit-setting process—which is so critical to healthy child development and healthy parent-child relationships—just another power struggle.

They engage Nico in being problem-solving partners. Nico is resistant to having reflective discussions, so I propose a strategy that has worked for many families: to have a "meeting," in person or via video call, to work on problem-solving. I came up with this idea during COVID when kids were constantly competing with their parents' video calls and thought it might be helpful to co-opt this medium. Kids wanted to have grown-up meetings, too, not just "stupid Zoom school" as one child called it. I wondered if connecting "remotely," without the intensity of being face-to-face, would be intriguing to kids and also provide a physical boundary that would make them feel more comfortable opening up.

I suggest parents introduce this concept by explaining to their children that the video calls they have with their colleagues are to solve problems together, and that families are problem-solving teams, too, so they will be setting up some video meetings. Each participant will be in their own meeting space (not in the same room). Accordingly, Chris and Amanda tell Nico that once a week before the bedtime routine they are going to have an important "meeting" via video to solve problems. They will take turns deciding on the issue they will focus on. Everyone will share their ideas and then mom and dad will come up with a plan. This is important to be clear about—that kids get to share their ideas, but moms and dads are in charge of making the final decision. They acknowledge that Nico wants to be in charge, so he may not like this. They don't expect him to and aren't asking him to, but that is the way families work.

Battles over Greek School

The Plan

Amanda and Chris start by telling Nico that Greek School is a "have-to," not a choice. They know he may not like that decision, and that is okay, they don't expect him to and aren't asking him to agree with it—that's a mommy/daddy decision. But they want to hear what he doesn't like about it. Nico responds that it's boring and stupid, the teacher is old and not funny, and the snacks are yucky. Amanda and Chris ask him to rank these complaints starting with the most annoying, which starts to put Nico in a more playful, positive mood. Chris tells stories of his own experience in Greek School and how he sometimes felt the same way. He explains that since it was also a have-to in his family, his parents created a ritual that on Greek School days, they added a fun "extra" to acknowledge the extra work he had put in: they had an indoor picnic for dinner and a movie night together. Nico loves this idea and asks if they can do that, too. Bingo! This is an effective way to address a child's desire to "equalize." You bake into the plan a benefit to show them there is a positive outcome for cooperating.

As for getting Nico to Greek School, they know they can't make him agree to get into the car and don't feel comfortable or able to move him there given his age and size, so they decide on the following plan that they share with him, so he knows exactly what to expect and what his choices are. They will use a visual timer so he can see exactly when they are leaving for Greek School. When the buzzer goes off, they will wait at the front door for him. They won't nag, bribe, or threaten. They will just wait. His two great choices will be: (1) to get into the car on time, which will add ten minutes to his daily screen time because cooperating and doing his job saves time for "extras"; (2) not to cooperate with leaving on time, which will deduct five minutes from screen time for every minute he makes them wait. By not telling him what to do, they are not giving him fodder for a fight.

The Outcome

The first day they implement this plan, Nico isn't ready when the timer goes off. Amanda, who is on Greek School duty, doesn't say a word. She just stands by the door and distracts herself by looking at her phone. Nico starts to get very silly; he runs around making nonsense noises and uses potty language. Kids are conflicted in these moments: part of them wants to do the right thing and cooperate, but another part of them wants to assert their independence and not cave to their parents' directions. This puts them in an uncomfortable position, hence the silliness. Critically, Amanda doesn't react, as that would only reinforce this behavior and divert her from the plan. Amanda has also learned not to count the passing minutes aloud, as that is very triggering for Nico—he gets hyper-focused on it, and it sends him into further dysregulation. After about four minutes, he runs past her out the door and climbs into the car. Again, with great attunement, Amanda doesn't say anything about how happy she is that he's cooperating. Why? Because Nico, like many kids I work with, has been known to do an immediate about-face when he doesn't want to eat crow—to indicate in any way, shape, or form that he is acquiescing to others' demands. You say that you love how they are cleaning up and they start to throw the toys. You say how happy you are that they are peeing on the potty and they purposefully pee on the floor.

When it's time for Nico's sixty minutes of screen time later that day, Amanda lets him know that it will be forty minutes because she had to wait four minutes after the timer went off for him to go to the car. Four multiplied by five equals twenty minutes. As expected, Nico starts to argue. Amanda doesn't respond to his protests. She just puts the timer on for forty minutes and tells him that this is his time to either use the tablet or not—that's up to him. She will be putting the tablet away when the timer goes off regardless of how he chooses to use the time. Nico continues to try to draw Amanda into a struggle. She feels herself getting triggered and tells Nico that this is uncomfortable for her so she's going to take a mommy moment to get calm. She goes into her room. He shouts at her through the door. She responds that the timer is still going, and he can decide to be angry or to use it for his screen time. Nico harrumphs and goes back to the tablet, shouting along the way, "You are the worst mommy," which Amanda ignores.

Taking this approach requires a heroic amount of self-control for both Chris and Amanda. But the payoff is huge. When they stay the course, don't engage in the power struggle, and set limits they have the power to implement, there are way fewer battles over Greek School. And they have a lovely new ritual in the dinner picnic and movie night.

Coping with the Unexpected

The Plan

Chris and Amanda show compassion for the fact that Nico doesn't like surprises. They recall times when he has fallen asleep on the way home from school and was very upset upon awakening unexpectedly in their driveway; or, when they have shown up for school pick-up or an activity with a snack he did not expect or want. They explain that while these situations are uncomfortable for him, they will happen because Chris and Amanda can't control everything. Their job is to help Nico cope in these moments. They won't drive all the way back to the spot where he had fallen asleep; they won't go home and get a new snack and then come all the way back to the school.

They brainstorm ideas for how they can help Nico in these situations. Amanda suggests that if he falls asleep on the way home from school—which does happen on occasion—they will drive around the block once to give him time to adjust to being back home. Nico adds that they could put on his favorite audiobook to listen to while they go around the block. Amanda loves this idea as it may also make it easier for Nico to transition into the house as he will be focused on something pleasurable.

As for snacks, they will plan them together so Nico will know what they are bringing when they pick him up from school or take him to an activity. If he still ends up rejecting that snack, he won't be getting a different one. They ask Nico what might help in those situations. He asks if he can pick a different snack once they get back home. They say of course, within limits; they are clear they can't give him sweet treats before dinner. They suggest making a list of all the healthy options he can choose from when he gets home. They call them "appetizers." Nico likes this idea.

The Outcome

Controlling car rides. Sticking to this approach requires Amanda and Chris to tolerate a lot of distress. The first time Nico falls asleep on the way home from school, he doesn't accept the idea of just going around the block and putting on his favorite audiobook. Amanda acknowledges his discomfort and sits with him calmly and quietly as he begs her to take him back to the spot where he fell asleep. Amanda resists trying to convince him to accept the tools they had agreed on. She remains a quiet presence. Within five minutes Nico starts to calm and asks for the audiobook.

Once they are in the house and Nico is no longer in distress, Amanda suggests that they think about ways to help him stay awake on these rides. They land on the idea of making up a story together, with each of them adding one idea at a time to weave the tale. More often than not, this works and becomes another lovely ritual they share.

The plan for snacks works well pretty quickly. Knowing his parents won't be engaging in arguments with him about it, and having plan B—that he can choose a different snack once they get home—reduces battles. But then there is an incident where Nico has a total meltdown when the restaurant that they go to doesn't make mac and cheese the way he likes it—there is too much "brown" on top. Amanda and Chris try to help him solve the problem—offering him a spoon to scrape off the part off that he doesn't like. But Nico rejects their attempts to help and further escalates. Chris ends up having to take Nico to the car for a break when he gets disruptive in this public setting. He acknowledges Nico's distress. At the same time, he explains that restaurants have rules for behavior. When someone is having a hard time following those rules, they need to find a safe place where they can get calm. With dad remaining a quiet presence, not reacting to Nico's protestations and accusations, he eventually calms. They return to the table and Nico accepts a different food.

Note: Amanda and Chris used to bring Nico's preferred foods to restaurants. But they decided that adapting to him in this way would not serve him well down the road. While this experience was very difficult and required incredible self-regulation on their part, it resulted in exactly what they are working toward—helping Nico learn to be flexible.

Overall, Amanda and Chris accept that even when they have done so much loving prevention, and have offered so many supportive tools, there are times when they will just have to weather the storm.

Responding in this way ultimately leads to fewer meltdowns and more adaptation.

Unbending Uma

The Presenting Problem

Jenny and Thomas seek my guidance about their two-year-old, Uma, who falls apart whenever something happens in a way that she doesn't like or expect: a puzzle is on the wrong shelf, they moved a chair from her room to another place; or Thomas doesn't sing the song he made up exactly the same way he did the night before. One of Uma's biggest triggers is when her mom wears her hair up in a ponytail, bun, or braid. She gets hysterical and demands that Jenny take it down immediately.

Jenny and Thomas are confused and very distressed by these reactions. They are also exhausted. Prior to starting our consultation, they had been racing to undo anything that made Uma uncomfortable. They moved the puzzle to the correct bookshelf. Thomas tried over and over to recreate the song exactly as Uma recalled it (which was impossible and concluded with a twenty-minute meltdown), and Jenny acquiesced to Uma's hairstyle demands and wore it down all the time. While they instinctively knew that constantly accommodating Uma's demands wasn't healthy, they just wanted her to be happy. They hoped and told themselves that she would grow out of it. But when it didn't get better, they called for a consult.

It's important to add that Uma does great at and loves school. Her teachers report that they don't see the inflexibility Jenny and Thomas are reporting and are surprised to hear about how differently she behaves at home. At school, she is very cooperative and content. (This is a very common phenomenon in the families I work with—a child who's a "superstar" at school and a "terror" at home—which I address, in depth in chapter 8.)

The Analysis

It becomes clear that Jenny and Thomas's hope that Uma would become more adaptable as she grows older is not happening. In fact, she is becoming more demanding and inflexible—making increasingly rigid demands about every step of their daily routines, such as how her owl babies are organized before bed, which can take up to thirty minutes. They are also getting very frustrated and short with her due to her increasing need for (seemingly irrational) rituals that are controlling their daily lives. They are feeling a lot more frustration and despair than connection and joy.

We also take into consideration that at school, Uma is able to be flexible; with clear structure and rules, she is able to adapt. Our job is to help her be able to flex that muscle at home too.

With this insight, Jenny and Thomas are ready and motivated to stop doing so much accommodating and to set appropriate limits to help Uma learn to cope when things don't happen exactly the way she expects or is comfortable with.

The Plan

They decide to start with Uma's fixation on Jenny's hair having to be down. The goal is to help Uma see Jenny as the trusted, adored mom she is no matter what her hair looks like. To that end, Jenny will not take her hair down on command and tolerates Uma's distress. They will then apply a similar approach to other situations in which Uma is being rigid in order to build her overall flexibility.

The Outcome

When Uma insists that mom take her hair down, Jenny responds: "I know, you like mommy's hair down, but mommy gets to decide how to wear my hair, and right now I'm more comfortable with it up. Remember, I am the same mama no matter how I wear my hair." Jenny rubs Uma's back and repeats in a loving voice, "Same mama."

After several weeks of this course correction, most of the time when Uma sees Jenny's hair is up, she gets a twinkle in her eye and says, "Same mama," which, understandably, makes Jenny tear up. It's so poignant. When Uma does melt down, Jenny responds, "I see it still sometimes makes you uncomfortable when mom's hair is up. I understand. Remember, 'same mama.'" Then Jenny stays quiet and present and gives Uma space to work it through. Uma eventually calms and moves on.

Muscling through this and experiencing the incredible sense of joy at having helped Uma overcome this significant challenge empowers Jenny and Thomas to apply the same approach to other similar dynamics with Uma. When Uma has to accept something the way it is, like mom having her hair up or the restaurant not having the kind of juice she wants, they show empathy and then give her space to work through the distress. "I know it's hard when they don't have the juice you like. You can choose another drink or not have a drink, that's up to you."

When Uma flips out because they move a chair from her room to another place where it is needed, Jenny and Thomas resist the urge to let it stay in Uma's room to avoid the meltdown. Instead, they acknowledge Uma's discomfort and displeasure with this change and try to brainstorm what they might put in its place. Uma is not ready to focus on solving this problem. She continues to cry and protest. They respond, "We're happy to think of other things to put in your room when you are ready," to signal that they aren't going to engage in a power struggle over this or change their minds. Once Uma sees they are holding firm, she starts to look at the pictures of other options her parents have curated. She ultimately decides on a beanbag chair, which soon becomes her preferred place for reading at bedtime.

When Uma is distressed over Thomas not recalling the exact words to a song he made up previously, he suggests they make up a new funny song together and write all the words down so they can remember them. Initially, Uma rejects this and throws herself on the floor in despair. When Thomas remains a quiet presence and doesn't try to make it all better, she pops up and agrees to the plan. They have a blast with the joint songwriting endeavor.

Making this major shift in their response to Uma is life-changing for all of them. She is becoming more flexible and there is so much more peace and joy. Jenny and Thomas are no longer walking on eggshells, now that they have tools to both deal with Uma's meltdowns and help her become her own best problem-solver.

SHORT STORIES

When Your Child Is Irrationally Inflexible

Amelia (four) is a highly sensitive child. She has big reactions when something doesn't appear the way she expects. On this occasion, Amelia asks her dad, Alan, for an apricot (a fresh one). When she cuts it open, she says it looks "gross and yucky" and refuses to eat it. (It is perfectly fine, not rotten.) Alan acknowledges Amelia's displeasure with the way it looks and explains that the same fruit can look different from piece to piece. Amelia continues to protest, demands a new apricot, and tells dad to take the "gross" one away—she doesn't want to touch it. Alan says he will give her a napkin to move the apricot on her own if she'd like. She takes it and moves it to the kitchen counter and continues to demand a new apricot. Amelia's badgering escalates. Alan acknowledges her displeasure with his choice—he understands and that's okay—but he's not going to change his decision. She can keep asking—it's her voice and only she controls it—but he is not going to keep discussing it. He distracts himself fussing around in the kitchen. He starts talking about a funny video he saw with dogs and offers to show it to her, to convey that he is not ignoring her, or mad or frustrated. He is being her rock. Within a few minutes, when Amelia sees that Alan is holding firm, she takes a bite of the apricot and announces, "This is the best apricot I've ever had!" as she gobbles it down.

While I see huge successes when parents take this approach, it doesn't always result in the child accepting whatever it is they had been rejecting. That doesn't mean this strategy is a failure. The win is that it avoids the power struggle and communicates that you believe their child can handle it when things don't happen or look the way they want. Staying this course makes it more likely your child will overcome their discomfort. Limits scaffold adaptation.

When Your Child Controls for Power and Control's Sake

Elliot (six) insists his mom, Megan, make him two sandwiches: a grilled cheese *and* peanut butter. Megan knows he will never eat both, so tells him he can choose one. A battle ensues for more than fifteen minutes. Elliot makes all sorts of arguments, including weaponizing an important message Megan frequently communicates: "You always tell me it's my body, and that I know what my body needs. Well, right now my body needs two sandwiches!" Megan keeps trying to defend the limit and to convince Elliot to accept one sandwich. The longer this goes on, the more heated and agitated they both get. At one point, Elliot threatens to turn on the stove and make his own grilled cheese sandwich. This is very triggering to Megan, who physically tries to move him away from the stove. Elliot starts screaming, "You're hurting me!" as he runs out of the room. At this point, Megan makes him both sandwiches. He comes back into the kitchen, takes one bite of one sandwich and runs off to play. Megan is beside herself.

In analyzing this dynamic—which plays out in countless ways each week—Megan sees that getting into these battles with Elliot is detrimental to both of them, and the whole family, and that it's reinforcing his inflexibility and demanding behavior. This motivates Megan to work on sticking to limits that will build Elliot's ability to adapt, which she knows will necessitate tolerating his distress, threats, and accusations. She takes the following steps:

She starts with empathy. If Megan had a redo of the sandwich incident, she would respond: "That was a tough moment for us. I am still working on how to be the best mom to you and help you cope when things don't go exactly the way you like. I know you wanted two sandwiches. Both grilled cheese and peanut butter are yummy and it's hard to decide which you want. We also can't be wasteful and throw food away. So next time that happens, I will make one sandwich. If you eat that one and are still hungry, I am happy to make you another one. We can even make that first sandwich half grilled cheese and half peanut butter."

She avoids negotiations. When a similar scenario comes up about having to make a choice in a toy store about which action figure to get, Megan implements the new approach. She does not engage in the negotiation Elliot is trying to draw her into to convince her to get both figures. She has told him he can choose one and will give him three minutes to make a choice. Elliot keeps trying to draw her in. She resists reacting; she just shows him the timer. When it goes off, he is still screaming at her and has not made a choice. She sticks to the limit and has to guide him out of the store. She tells him that she is happy to try again the next day if he wants.

She doesn't get defensive. Elliot remains angry for the entire rest of the day, which is very wearing, but Megan doesn't react. She keeps reminding herself that he is a great kid having a difficult moment and that she is helping him build resilience and flexibility. All she says is, "I know, it was a tough day. Making choices can be really hard." Then right before bed, Elliot asks if they can go back to the store the next day. Megan says they can and offers to help him think through which action figure he wants to choose, so when they get to the store it might be easier. He immediately leans into this idea.

The Outcome

When they go back to the store, Elliot runs to the shelf and grabs one action figure and happily skips to the register. He is in a great mood for the rest of the day. In fact, Megan senses an overall change in Elliot. This is a pattern I often see: when kids learn to be flexible, it has an overarching, positive impact on them. They are less agitated in general and less fierce about the fight, which is so exhausting for kids and parents. They seem more relaxed and content. This is a good reminder that what feels mean (not giving your child exactly what they want) is often loving.

When Your Child Makes Irrational Demands

Arthur and Hadley are distressed about the constant power struggles with their son, Ryder (seven). They send me audio of a difficult encounter so I can hear exactly how these scenarios unfold and help them figure out what they can do differently. In this case, at bedtime, Ryder is insisting that he needs to go back downstairs after he is already in his room getting ready to read with Arthur before lights-out. Ryder proclaims that he doesn't want to read books. He wants to use his time to paint.

> Arthur: "Ryder, we are not doing art now. We are getting ready for bed. There is no going back downstairs."
> Ryder screams: "That's stupid. All you want me to do is read and read and read and read because you think it's educational. Well art is educational too. Haven't you ever heard of art class?"
> Arthur: "It's bedtime, which is reading time."
> Ryder: "That doesn't make any sense! You never let me do anything I want to do. This is the worst day ever!"
> Arthur: "That is not true, Ryder. You get to do so many things you want to do . . . [Arthur proceeds to remind Ryder of many recent examples]."

Arthur's repeated efforts to explain (defend) himself—to convince Ryder to see that his accusations are unfounded and that the limit is fair—are just fodder for Ryder to keep upping the ante. His retorts get fiercer and increasingly irrational: "You care more about Lilah [his younger sister] than me! She gets to do art whenever she wants! You are so mean to me. I don't even think you love me!" This goes on for more than twenty minutes, with Arthur playing defense, countering every accusation and negotiation point. He is completely worn down and ends up letting Ryder do art for an extra thirty minutes before lights-out. After we process this experience, Arthur makes the following course corrections:

In a quiet, not heated, moment, Arthur explains to Ryder the difference between a choice and a "have-to." Choices are decisions kids get to make, like what flavor ice cream they want, which shirt to wear, and what game to play. Have-tos are things that must happen to keep kids healthy and safe, like going to bed on time, being buckled in car seats, brushing their teeth, and getting to school on time. They brainstorm a list of what would go into each category. (Kids are generally keen on participating in this exercise when it is all in theory, not practice!)

Arthur acknowledges Ryder's feelings—that accepting limits, especially at bedtime, is hard. It's a mommy/daddy job to make rules that keep kids healthy. That's why the firm family rule is that after wash-up/bathroom time, kids go directly into their rooms where they stay until morning so they can calm their minds and bodies for sleep. Mom and dad will not allow playing or running around the house right before bed; those are daytime activities.

Both mom and dad tell Ryder that he will always have choices—in this case, about how he wants to spend his twenty minutes of quiet time in his room before lights-out: he can opt to read on his own or have one parent read to him. He can even spend the time drawing in his room; he just can't go downstairs and paint. They tell him that they love him so much they are not going to get into a fight about this. They acknowledge that they can't stop him from trying to negotiate, but they won't be responding. They are very confident about their rule and accept that Ryder may not be happy about it. They also explain that staying in his room after lights-out is a "have-to." How it happens is up to him. Option one is he follows the direction and stays in his room. Option two is he comes out, in which case they will use a door-helper to help him follow the rule. (See the appendix for resources on how to make a sleep plan that is loving and effective.)

The Outcome

The next night, after his shower, Ryder announces that he is fine not doing art that night. (Phew!) But when the twenty minutes of reading time are up, he insists Arthur keep reading because he cannot wait to know what happens next. Arthur acknowledges that it's really hard to stop reading at such an exciting moment, but going to bed now is a "have-to." Ryder immediately launches into furthering his case. (At one point, he offers his dad $5 to keep reading!)

Arthur doesn't respond to Ryder's accusations and pleas. He knows that it will just fuel the fire, and that not responding will signal that he will not be going down this rabbit hole with Ryder. Instead, Arthur says he is so excited to continue reading *Harry Potter* tomorrow and that he can't wait to see Ryder in the morning. Then Arthur leaves. Ryder shouts from his room for a good long time, but Arthur doesn't react. Ryder comes charging out of the room. Arthur takes Ryder back to his room as he quietly says: "No problem, I'll be a helper."

He uses the boundary they have chosen to secure the door closed to prevent Ryder from continuing to leave the room and promulgating a whole other pernicious and physical power struggle. Ryder continues to shout and protest from his room. After about ten minutes with no response, he settles and goes to sleep. After this episode, when his parents continue to be clear about the expectations and follow through on their limits, without engaging in debates and negotiations, bedtime battles and other scenarios with the same dynamic, abate. Most importantly, their special time together before bed—often the only time of day they have to slow down and truly connect—goes from being tense and fraught to being filled with joy and bonding.

FINAL THOUGHTS

As I analyze the kinds of interactions featured in this chapter with parents, it becomes evident that a foundational problem they share is a lack of a clear limits. Kids find a *loophole*: a vacuum created by the lack of a clear boundary that children, especially the fierce and feisty ones, fill. Once your child susses out that the limit you are trying to set is not firm but, rather, dependent on their agreement and cooperation, they expend an incredible amount of energy throwing up any and all possible obstacles to prevent the limit from being implemented. Who can blame them? I haven't yet met a child who was happy about handing over a tablet, accepting an apple as dessert instead of cookies, or having to end a joyful bedtime. They will negotiate and argue, making some very coherent but also some very irrational arguments and employ a whole host of delay tactics.

This intense focus on exploiting any opening they detect is hard work. It takes a lot of mental energy to refute all their parents' talking points and make their case about why the limit is unnecessary or even wrong. They accuse you of being mean: they never get enough time to play before dinner. You are being unfair: you let the older sibling stay up later. You are a bad parent: "Don't you know that it's illegal to ignore your child?" This was shouted at parents, both attorneys, who had said after lights-out they were not coming back into their child's room, even if he called out for them. And, of course, there's the guilt trip: the child accuses his mom of only making foods that she likes and not caring about what he likes, and so he is just going to starve.

The longer children are able to keep their parents engaged in these debates/battles, the more revved up and irrational they tend to get. This is exhausting for kids who expend a lot of mental energy making their case and pursuing all angles, getting themselves increasingly wound up and dysregulated. The entire situation escalates and everyone involved ends up miserable. It is also extremely exhausting for parents who find themselves getting drawn into constant negotiations and defending/justifying to their children why they are setting these important, necessary limits. They are also very frustrated and annoyed with their kids, which saddens them. It's not what leads to the loving connection they want and need with their kids.

While it feels manipulative and maddening, your kids are just very strategic and smart. They are doing what their DNA dictates—to pursue what *they want*: to have your attention twenty-four seven; to enjoy endless sweets and screentime; to have endless books at bedtime; to get the desired toy; or to stay home, in their comfort zone, instead of having to make a transition to school or an activity. It's up to us—as the adults guiding our children's way through the world—to figure out *what our kids need* and to set limits that ensure their healthiest development: to get the sleep their brains and bodies need, to get to school on time, to eat more healthy foods than junk foods, to learn to accept when they can't get what they want.

Alas, the kids who are the most controlling and inflexible need the most loving and firm limits. The absence of a clear boundary is what impedes their learning to be more adaptable and results in their spiraling further out of control. The take home: limits are loving, and happy children are not always happy.

4

Anxiety

Izzy [four] was a mess all week. She was on edge, falling apart more than usual over minor things she can typically handle. Then, at bedtime a few days into this very unpleasant period, she asked if she had to participate in her upcoming dance recital. I realized, then, that she had been stewing over this, and it was the cause of her angst all week. It all made sense.

Leon [seven] asks every night before bed what the weather is going to be. He wants to know if it's going to rain because, during a recent storm, a big tree limb fell on our neighbor's car and dented the roof. No one was hurt, but for days after it was all Leon could talk about. He asked myriad questions and expressed concern about what would happen if someone was in the car. Could they get hurt?

Anxiety is caused by feelings of uncertainty: not knowing what to expect and not being able to control the outcome. Thus, it is not surprising that highly sensitive children (HSCs) are more prone to anxiety and that it's at the root of many of their challenges. Their deep processing means their brains are working overtime, absorbing and trying to make sense of all the information and experiences they are exposed to. They take in more than they can handle. To guard against the unknown, they develop a range of coping strategies. They think ten steps ahead about what might happen in any given situation so they are not blindsided and can be prepared for anything. That is why HSCs have a strong need to know exactly what to expect—to avoid surprises.

To protect themselves from potential discomfort, HSCs make decisions—often unconscious—that guide their behavior: Sebby finally gets the courage to go down the slide. He does it several times with delight. Then, on one go-around, he bumps his bottom on the ground. He has refused to go on a slide since. ("Slide hurts. Slide bad. No more slide.") Jessie goes to a birthday party. Without warning, a swarm of people enter the room, birthday cake in hand, bursting out with the "Happy Birthday" song. She completely melts down, overwhelmed by this unexpected sensory experience. Ever since, Jessie not only refuses to go to birthday parties but is also terrified of candles. ("Birthday parties are overwhelming. No more birthday parties. Candles are at birthday parties. Must stay away from candles.") You can see how anxiety is an undercurrent and at play in many of the challenging behaviors with which HSCs struggle.

The Connection Between Anxiety and Self-Consciousness

Jonah is hesitant to go to swim class. He doesn't want the kids or teacher to look at him when it's his turn to do an exercise.

Miriam will only participate in school performances standing with her back to the audience or from behind the curtain. She instructs her parents not to clap.

HSCs are often keenly focused on how others see them. They get very uncomfortable when any attention is called to them, even when parents or other adults are praising them. They process praise as evaluation, which, in fact, it is. Others are watching them and assessing their performance. This translates into pressure that can result in paralysis. They sense that their performance has the power to please or disappoint others, especially their parent(s), which is overwhelming and stressful and shuts them down.

The Connection Between Anxiety and Irritability

Recall Izzy who had been in a foul mood for days leading up to her bedtime confession that she was worried about her upcoming dance recital. Many parents share similar scenarios. Their kids are more irritable and dysregulated than usual, sometimes for a few days. Then, often at bedtime, when kids are more open and their defenses are down, they blurt out the reason they are anxious. A four-year-old exclaims: "I don't want to move to the next [older children's] classroom." A five-year-old shares she is scared about taking a bus to school. If you notice your child going through a more dysregulated period, it can be helpful to explore what's on their mind. You might share: "When I am thinking a lot about something new that is happening in my life, or something I am worried about, I feel cranky. Do you ever feel that way? Is there anything your brain is thinking a lot about?"

The Connection Between Anxiety and a Child's Ability to Access Their Skills

How we behave is deeply influenced by our level of comfort in a situation. If I am presenting to a group of people whom I don't know and feel may be harsh critics and judgy, I am more halting and inarticulate and don't perform to my capacity. When I am with a group that I am familiar with and feel safe with, I am on top of my game. The same is true for kids. It may be that your child feels anxious in big groups and shuts down. Or they get overwhelmed when a lot is going on around them. They may be self-conscious and may not like "performing" for fear of being evaluated. They get anxious and become constricted and avoidant. They are not able to be their best, free, most confident, competent self.

In the beginning of a new school year, kids are often anxious about this big transition—either to a new program, teacher, classroom—or simply making the change from summer break back to school. All of their psychic energy is diverted to adapting to this new experience. Some skills go into regression or are subsumed and shut down, including not using the bathroom or eating at school. With time, as children get more comfortable, they relax and resume healthy bodily functions.

A child's performance can also be affected by anxiety. I often hear from parents that their child is a huge "ham" and doesn't stop talking at home; yet, at school or outside of home, the same child is very quiet and doesn't talk much. At home, a child may love to dance and sing, but, in music and dance class, they are hesitant hesitant to participate. They freeze up and don't feel free to engage the way they do at home—their comfort zone.

Anxiety is often at the core of why HSCs are prone to meltdowns, are demanding and inflexible, are cautious and in need of additional time to adapt to new situations, have a tough time with change, are perfectionists and sore losers, and struggle with self-consciousness and performance anxiety—all challenges addressed in this book. Providing the support your HSC needs to feel less anxious begins with some important mindshifts.

MINDSHIFTS

All stress is not equal. Stress is a part of life for all humans, and all stress is not the same or equal. The temporary distress children experience when confronting new situations or challenges—like starting school or a new activity—is what we, in the world of child development, call "positive stress."[1] These experiences are uncomfortable but not harmful. Unlike "toxic stress," which is caused by abuse, neglect, persistent shaming, and harsh punishment, "positive stress" leads to learning and growth. It is muscling through discomfort that leads to the development of new skills and builds resilience. Reminding yourself that the stress your child may experience as you help them face and overcome their fears is "positive stress" (also called "positive discomfort") is essential to successfully guiding them through this process.

What feels mean is sometimes loving. Helping your child manage their fears often requires exposing them to situations that cause anxiety. Putting your child in an expectedly stressful situation can feel straight-up mean. That's why it's crucial to remind yourself that doing so is a gift to your child, even when they are not making you feel like you are being loving.

Don't fear your child's feelings. This mindshift is key to every issue addressed in this book. When I first meet families struggling to handle their child's big feelings, they are frequently focused on trying to change those feelings. They don't want their child to feel sad, angry, jealous, or, in this case, anxious, because they worry it will inhibit healthy development. As noted previously, ignoring or minimizing feelings doesn't make them magically disappear. Kids up the ante to be heard. Example: you tell your child she doesn't have to be afraid of the pool—the instructor will be sure she doesn't drown, and she responds, "What if they aren't looking at me and are looking at another kid so they don't see me drowning?"

When children's feelings are understood and accepted, it ultimately opens them up to reflecting on their emotions and experiences, to think through their worries and ultimately change their perspective and thought process, as the cases below illustrate.

CASES

Izzy and Her Irritability

The Presenting Problem

Recall Izzy (four) who was anxious about her upcoming dance recital. Her parents, Melissa and Trevor, initially came to see me because of an uptick in meltdowns that are usually precipitated by situations Izzy can't control and that are new and uncomfortable for her—that is, when she can't anticipate what to expect. Recently, they went on a family vacation. For the first three days, Izzy was a complete mess; she couldn't cope with anything. The food wasn't right, the bed was too mushy, and the pool was too "wet." Then on day four, she turned a corner and had a blast. When they left on day six, Izzy announced that it was her favorite place in the world, and she couldn't wait to go back!

Izzy can also get very stuck, perseverating on a troubling incident. When she started school, she did great the first day. The second day she was more hesitant. An assistant from another class, Sarah, who happens to have bright red hair, comforted her. When Izzy wouldn't get up to walk to her class, Sarah carried her there, calmly and lovingly. Izzy had a big, negative reaction to being picked up. She became very anxious about school and started saying she didn't want to go. Her complaints would start the night before and continue throughout the morning routine and the drive to school. It has slowly gotten better; now Izzy is fine until they are in the car approaching the school, at which point she starts talking about not liking the "teacher with the red hair." Similarly, Izzy loves the community pool but has started resisting going after she witnessed a lifeguard whistle at some kids to signal to them to walk, not run.

Melissa and Trevor are wonderful, gentle parents who are very empathetic and supportive. They have been trying to help Izzy process all of these big feelings and reactions but find that the more they try to get her to talk about her emotions and experiences, the more agitated she becomes. They are not sure how to help her.

The Analysis

Melissa and Trevor share that Izzy has been a big reactor since birth. As soon as she started to talk, they knew she was an "old soul." By age two, she was already showing signs of being a deep processor. She keenly keyed into the nuances of everything and made profound statements, like telling her parents that the boy throwing mulch at the playground was sad, not bad, which he was because some kids had just told him he couldn't play with them.

Like most HSCs, Izzy doesn't like surprises and has a strong need to know what to expect and to feel in control, which made the incident with Sarah, the "teacher with the red hair," so distressing. She is also very self-conscious and has performance anxiety—common traits of HSCs due to their tendency to overanalyze. This leads to worry about what others think of them and explains Izzy's anxiety about the upcoming dance performance. She hates having any attention called to her. She shouts at her parents to stop talking when she hears them saying something about her, even when it's positive. When she does something they're proud of, she tells them not to clap for her. And the pool incident? The idea that a whistle could suddenly be blown at her—she hates sudden, loud noises—and could cause everyone to focus on her is terrifying.

The Plan

We work with the school to address Izzy's anxiety about Sarah, the red-haired assistant. We decide this is important because Izzy seems to have globalized this experience with one staff member to seeing school, overall, as "dangerous"—that is, at any moment she could be picked up and moved without warning or explanation. We know she doesn't like being touched when she is in distress; plus, being picked up felt sudden and surprising given her emotional state. It's fair to wonder why they didn't just wait until she had calmed. In theory, that might have worked. But the reality in schools, especially in the beginning of the year when many kids are anxious, is that having a child screaming in the middle of the lobby is very distressing to other children and creates a tense atmosphere. In group settings, we need to consider how to balance the needs of the individual child with the needs of the other kids in the group. Further, lovingly moving a child to a more contained, quiet space when they are unraveling can be a very supportive step and sometimes necessary.

The first step is for Becky, Izzy's teacher whom she adores and feels very secure with, to acknowledge that being picked up by Sarah was surprising and uncomfortable to Izzy. Becky explains that in the future, if Izzy ever needs help to be moved somewhere, they will always give her the choice to go on her own. If she can't, because sometimes kids are very upset and aren't able to move themselves, an adult will let her know they are going to help her move so she is not surprised.

They also implement a plan to incrementally and sensitively expose Izzy to Sarah in situations that show how warm, loving, and safe Sarah is, for example, taking the class to the playground when Sarah is out there. Becky talks to Izzy about what she sees Sarah doing with the other kids that is so fun. Becky also invites Sarah to be a guest reader in the class because Izzy *loves* books. Becky hopes this will serve as an icebreaker.

Melissa and Trevor talk to Izzy about her "worry brain" and "thinking brain." They use the incident at the pool as an example. They acknowledge that Izzy doesn't like attention called to her or being corrected. When she heard the lifeguard blow the whistle at the kids who were running, her "worry brain" took over and decided that she should never go back to the pool to prevent that unpleasant experience from ever happening to her. What might her "thinking brain" tell her? They remind Izzy that she has total control over her body; she chooses whether or not to run. If she follows the rules, the lifeguard won't have to blow his whistle at her.

They suggest being detectives to see if "thinking brain" is correct; can she be in charge of how her body moves? They agree to investigate this at their local playground, a safer spot for Izzy. Izzy loves this idea. They also acknowledge that while Izzy doesn't like to be corrected and tries to do everything "right," she is a human, and as humans, we all make mistakes and need guidance. That guidance was what the lifeguard was providing—he wasn't angry at the kids, and they weren't in trouble—he was just reminding them of the rule to walk, not run. He was being a helper. This is a very important message for kids, especially those who are terrified of doing something wrong: mistakes are expected, and adults are there to help them make healthy choices.

They amend how they respond to Izzy's performance anxiety. Melissa and Trevor had previously been trying to encourage and motivate Izzy when she was feeling self-conscious and hesitant to participate in any kind of performance. When she shunned their praise, they tried to convince her that she should be happy that they are proud of her accomplishments.

With these new insights about Izzy—that even the slightest coaxing or encouragement can cause her to retreat and make it less likely she will feel comfortable performing—they change course. Now when Izzy reveals that she is anxious about an upcoming dance recital, instead of cheerleading, Melissa asks Izzy if she wants mom to tell the story of how recitals go. Melissa knows that Izzy is a processor and has found that previewing—telling the story of what to expect in a new situation—helps Izzy gain some control over it. She is optimistic that this will help with her anxiety about the recital.

The Outcome

School anxiety. When Izzy sees Sarah on the playground, she is cautious but interested. She watches Sarah playing with students and inches incrementally closer. Sarah invites Izzy to join in, but she's not ready. She just wants to be a watcher at this point.

When Sarah reads to Izzy's class, Izzy starts by sitting on her teacher's lap in the back. Sarah is dramatic and actively engages the kids in acting out parts of the story. Izzy ultimately joins in. By the end of this special reading time, Sarah gives all the kids high fives. When she gets to Sarah, she asks if she wants to give a high five or a wave. Izzy hesitates and then gently taps Sarah's hand up high. These interventions result in a significant reduction in Izzy's anxiety about going to school.

The pool. At the playground, Melissa and Trevor play a game with Izzy that entails them cuing her to walk, skip, or run so Izzy can test out if "thinking" brain is correct. Can she make her body follow the correct direction? She can! Izzy has the best time with this "practice" and is game to try it out at the pool, which is also a success. Melissa and Trevor also talk to the lifeguard about having a meeting with Izzy so she can ask all her questions about the pool rules—another intervention that Izzy loves. It humanizes the lifeguard and greatly eases Izzy's anxiety.

The dance recital. Izzy is keen on hearing the story of how the recital will go and asks Melissa to repeat the story, night after night, for an entire week. Melissa doesn't ask anything about the upcoming dress rehearsal or recital, as she knows that this will be interpreted as pressure—that mom is invested in and wanting Izzy to participate and will be disappointed if she doesn't.

After her next dance class, Izzy spontaneously announces that they had the dress rehearsal. Again, Melissa knows less is more—that a big, excited reaction may result in total retreat and shut down by Izzy. She responds with a simple "Oh" to convey interest without any expectation. Izzy responds: "I did it! I did the practice dance!" In a follow-up consult, Melissa reports that after the dress rehearsal, Izzy was excited the entire week leading up to the recital. She and Trevor continued to not make a big deal out of it. They just reflected back Izzy's excitement without conveying any expectations.

The outcome? Melissa recounts:

> *Izzy performed at the recital, and she was amazing. I was so emotional watching her because I was so happy for her. She was so conflicted about it—she clearly wanted to do it so badly and had to fight through the self-consciousness. The best part was seeing how proud she was of herself. She still didn't want praise and attention, but I knew she felt really good. She's been wearing her costume and playing her recital song on repeat since the performance, and she is asking when dance class starts up again. So much success!*

Melissa and Trevor also share another indication that Izzy is feeling less anxious, overall. They explain that Izzy loves to make up elaborate pretend scenarios. She always plays the role of an older child, a fairy, or a superhero—they assume, to feel powerful. She directs her mom and dad to play the role of Izzy. For months, the situations she had been playing out were all perilous, such as fires, the school door being locked, or someone being sick. Recently they have noticed that the scenarios have morphed from scary to more mundane situations— like going on a picnic or a treasure hunt. Pretend is a powerful way children work through their fears and is a strong sign that Izzy is feeling less anxious.

Fiona and the Fear of Flooding

The Presenting Problem

Rob and Martin come to see me because their daughter, Fiona (five), was refusing to use the bathroom in her kindergarten classroom. This was precipitated by an incident that happened the week before: the toilet overflowed when Fiona flushed it. The other kids found it funny, but Fiona was very distressed by it. She kept saying she was afraid of the toilet and the water. It took a long time for her teachers to console her. They ultimately helped Fiona calm by telling her she didn't have to go anywhere near the bathroom. Now, when she needs something from her cubby, which is close to the bathroom, they get it for her. They have to get an assistant from the office to take her to another bathroom.

The Analysis

Rob and Martin share that Fiona is a very sensitive child who notices and reacts strongly to any and all changes in her environment. She has a fierce need to control everything and hates the unexpected. When they move a piece of furniture, she gets very upset and demands it go back to where it was. When a food doesn't look the way she expects, she refuses to eat it. When they go downstairs one morning and there is a new doorman, she gets very upset, won't greet him, sometimes even growls at him, and won't let him hold the door for her.

Given Fiona's significant discomfort with the unexpected, her response to the toilet flooding is not surprising. Her brain immediately goes into "flight"[2] mode to protect herself from this deeply uncomfortable experience. Her coping mechanism is to avoid ever going near that bathroom again. This makes sense when you look at it from her perspective. The problem is twofold: (1) This is very hard for the school—they don't always have an extra adult who can escort Fiona to another bathroom; and (2) these are missed opportunities to help Fiona work through this fear and support her ability to adapt when something unexpected happens.

The Plan

Rob and Martin start by engaging in reflective conversations with Fiona about what makes her tick to build her self-awareness. They start by acknowledging how her amazing brain figures out so many things and that she really likes to know what to expect. When something surprising happens, it's very uncomfortable for her. They get that, and their job is to help her with it because we can't control everything that happens in the world.

They tell the story of what happened with the toilet to help her gain mastery over it. "You made your pee. You flushed the toilet like you always do, but this time, instead of the water going down, it came up. That was very surprising and uncomfortable because it's not what your brain was expecting. You ran out of the bathroom to get away from the water. The other kids laughed because they thought it was funny to see water come out of the toilet. [They add this because Fiona thought the kids were laughing at her at the time.] Ms. Marnie, your teacher, came in and cleaned it up. She called the front office for help. Someone came and fixed the toilet. The water doesn't come out anymore."

They do experiments that help sensitize Fiona to similar events. Most involve liquids flowing out of cups, bowls, and other receptacles, including making a volcano. They start by having Fiona control when it erupts. Then, they play a game in which Rob and Martin make the volcano overflow at unexpected moments.

They do research. Together with Fiona, they go onto the internet and learn about why toilets overflow and what can be done to prevent it from happening. They learn that putting things other than toilet paper can clog it. Fiona comes up with the idea to ask the teacher to tell all the kids that only toilet paper goes in the "potty." They also research what happens when toilets overflow—do people get hurt by it? Thankfully, the Worldwide Web reports that people don't get harmed by overflowing toilets, and that these incidents only happen when flushing, not spontaneously while people are sitting on them!

They have the "worry brain" versus "thinking brain" discussion. Fiona's "worry brain" has made a decision that the toilet is unsafe, and she should stay away from it. What does her "thinking brain" know? Since the person came to fix the toilet, it hasn't overflowed. They have the plan in place for the teacher to be sure the kids don't put objects other than toilet paper into the toilet. The research they have done has shown that toilets don't overflow when people are sitting on them, only when they are flushed. And overflowing toilets aren't dangerous—they don't cause harm to people.

Ms. Marnie helps Fiona take incremental steps to approach the toilet. She explains that they are going to be investigators to see what they can learn about the toilet. Ms. Marnie's job is to test the toilet first thing in the morning to see if it's working properly. When Fiona arrives at school, Ms. Marnie will report what she has learned when Fiona arrives at school. Ms. Marnie will check it again while Fiona stands outside the stall. After Ms. Marnie flushes, it's Fiona's job to check to see if it floods.

Rob, Martin and the teacher help Fiona plan what to do if the toilet floods again. Fiona comes up with the idea to wear her rain boots because one thing she really didn't like was her feet getting wet. (She had been wearing open sandals.) As cumbersome as this seems, she brings a pair of boots to school and keeps them in her cubby. The idea is to empower Fiona with tools that will help her feel more in control if something like this happens again, to reduce her anxiety.

The Outcome

Fiona is very eager to hear her dads tell the story of the toilet overflowing and asks them to repeat it frequently. She chimes in several times with, "They weren't laughing at me, they were laughing at the water!" This is a clear signal that feeling self-conscious and shame about the incident had been a significant factor and that correcting this interpretation was very important.

She loves the experiments, especially when Rob and Martin do the surprise volcano eruptions. She asks them to do this over and over. Rob and Martin can see that these "safe surprises" are therapeutic; that they're helping her master her fear. Further proof of her working through her worry is that when they watch *Aladdin* and ask Fiona what her wish would be, she responds: "For all the potties in the world to flood," and then she starts cracking up. Making fun of something scary can be a very powerful, effective coping mechanism for overcoming fears.

At school, Fiona takes to the idea of being an investigator. Ms. Marnie adds a nice touch of giving Fiona a notepad to jot down her observations. She makes two columns on the pages—one with a "Yes" written at the top and the other with a "No." If the toilet floods, Fiona's job is to put a checkmark in the "Yes" column. If it doesn't flood, she puts a checkmark in the "No" column. At the end of the day, her job is to add up the checkmarks and report her findings to Ms. Marnie, sharing her conclusion about whether the bathroom is safe or not. It's always safe. Ms. Marnie also helps Fiona and a few peers make a poster to put on the bathroom stall. It has two circles: one with a picture of a toilet paper roll inside a big green circle with a smiley face, and then another red circle that has objects that can't go into the toilet, like paper towels and wrappers, with a big red line across it.

After three days of Ms. Marnie implementing these strategies, Fiona says she is ready to try again. She puts on her rain boots and asks Ms. Marnie to come in and flush for her after she is out of the stall. From there, they move to Fiona being in the stall but right next to the open door when Ms. Marnie flushes. Ultimately, they switch positions; Fiona flushes and Ms. Marnie stands by the door. Then one day, Fiona walks into the stall without putting on her rain boots, uses the toilet, and flushes on her own. She runs out of the bathroom into Ms. Marnie's arms and shouts, "I did it!"

Rob and Martin implement similar steps for Fiona's other fears. She is now putting her head underwater at the pool and playing on her own in the basement (previously she had insisted an adult be there with her). They also see a reduction in her fears, overall.

SHORT STORIES

Fear of the Unknown

Owen is a very cautious three-year-old. He is wild about Daniel Tiger, so his parents, Ruth and Evan, buy tickets to see the live show. While Owen was ecstatic in theory, on the way to the event he becomes increasingly anxious, asking all sorts of questions about what will happen at the show. By the time they arrive, Ruth and Ethan don't know if Owen will make it. They are prepared for him to insist they turn around, which has been known to happen in similar situations. Then, a lightbulb goes off in Ruth's head: she gets down on Owen's eye level and asks what would make him feel better. He says he wants to know exactly how the show will start—what will be the very first thing that happens. Ruth locates someone from the production who explains to Owen, play-by-play, how the show will open. With this information, Owen becomes calm and proceeds to fully enjoy the show. (Ethan, who recounted this story to me, described this move on his wife's part as no less monumental than splitting the atom.)

Rumi Running the Show

Rumi (seven) won't go anywhere in her house alone. She insists that her mom, Myra, be in the bathroom with her while she's bathing, in her bedroom when she's getting dressed, and in the basement to play. Rumi is fine outside the home. She does great at school. Myra isn't sure if it's a true fear or if it's just a way to get all of mom's attention. Either way, it's not sustainable. Rumi has two younger brothers and they have a very busy household. Myra doesn't know how to help Rumi with this. She wants to be supportive, but she also needs to be a mom to *all* her kids. We come up with this plan:

- Myra talks to Rumi about her "worry brain" and "thinking brain." It's hard for Rumi to put into words what she's afraid of. Myra helps her go through each worry and recruit thinking brain to check on worry brain's fears: the house is safe—the doors are locked, and they don't allow strangers in; Rumi is able to get safely out of the bath, there is a stepping stool there to help.

- We come up with a plan for Rumi to take the baby video monitor with her when she goes into a room separate from mom so Myra can stay connected. Rumi knows mom can see her and that all is well.

- In a quiet moment, Myra explains to Rumi that she has important mommy jobs that need to get done for everyone in the family. And Rumi has her own jobs, like bathing and getting dressed independently. When Rumi does her jobs on her own, and doesn't need Myra to stay with her, it saves Myra time, which means they can have more time for fun activities—something we suspect is a big factor and motivator. If she does all her bathroom tasks on her own at night, Myra can add five minutes to their reading and cuddle time. When Rumi gets dressed on her own in the morning, Myra has time to sit with her at breakfast and tell a story from her childhood—something Rumi especially loves. When Myra has to be with Rumi when she does the jobs she is capable of doing independently, there is less time for fun connection because Myra has to make up that time doing her other jobs for the family

This plan moves the needle in a big way. Rumi is very motivated to have more special time with mom, which helps her override her fear and experience that she is safe on her own in the home: a huge positive for

Rumi (and mom!). The video monitor helps a lot. We ultimately have to put some limits on its use because Rumi wants to constantly talk to Myra when she needs to be talking to the other kids! They move to five-minute check-ins. At some point, they switch out the video monitor for a Bluetooth speaker. They use it to play audio recordings she has made with Rumi of them reading books and singing together. As Rumi starts to act much more confidently and independently at home, Myra has noticed a sizeable shift in her demeanor. She is less irritable and much more joyful.

FINAL THOUGHTS

It's important to note that there are times when a child's anxiety is interfering with their ability to participate in daily routines and activities and is negatively affecting their overall, healthy functioning. The rituals they insist on may have become too cumbersome—for example, a bedtime routine extends for hours as your child demands that you repeat a series of steps in exactly the same way night after night and the list becomes longer and longer. Or your child's worries are all-encompassing and pervasive, and they are going to extremes to avoid any discomfort—making their worlds very small. If this is the case, I strongly recommend that you seek professional guidance as even the most supportive, skilled parenting may not be enough.

5

Cautious and Slow to Warm Up

Jasper (five) loves the water and playing in the pool. But every time his parents, Rena and David, talk to him about taking a swimming class, he flat out refuses. They think it's important that Jasper learn to swim for safety reasons and so find themselves in a bind: they know they can't make him agree to take the classes but worry about him missing out on fun events with his peers and learning new skills that would bring him pleasure and build his confidence.

Rena and David have been around this block before with Jasper, who avoids doing any extracurricular activities. His preferred activity is playing at home. It's like pulling teeth even to get him to go to a family friend's home for a get-together. They don't know what to do—how to get him to agree to participate in activities that they are confident he would enjoy if he would only give them a chance.

Jasper is a highly sensitive child, and, like many highly sensitive children (HSCs), he is hesitant about trying new things. Common stories from parents include:

- "Mila [five] loves gymnastics, but every time there are new kids in the class, or they introduce new equipment, she clings to me and begs to go home."
- "Bodie [four] loves the library, but when I try to take him to story time, he won't sit with the other kids and runs away. He just wants me to read to him in a separate space. I feel bad that he can't enjoy this experience that all the other kids are clearly loving, but I don't know how to make him participate. What's wrong with him?"

As Dr. Elaine Aron, author of *The Highly Sensitive Child*,[1] explains, HSCs have a strong "pause to check system" in place. Being the deep processors that they are, when they enter a new situation, their brains work furiously to figure out what it's all about. Whether it's entering a new classroom, going to a birthday party, swim class or other group activity—their wheels are turning. They wonder: *What is this place? What will happen here? Who are these people? What can I expect from them? Will they like me? Will I be safe? Will I be good at whatever is expected of me here?*

This intense scrutiny takes a lot of emotional energy and can feel overwhelming, resulting in a knee-jerk reaction to avoid new situations altogether to protect themselves from the discomfort they experience when they don't know exactly what to expect. When you see it from their perspective, it makes sense that they may fight fiercely to stay in their comfort zone, which often means home. For HSCs, the connection between being slow to warm up and prone to anxiety becomes clear.

MINDSHIFTS

The following shifts in thinking have helped many families support their children to muscle through the discomfort of learning to adapt to new or challenging experiences.

All stress is not equal. As noted in chapter 3 on anxiety, stress is a part of life for all humans, and all stress is not the same or equal. The temporary distress children experience when confronting new situations or challenges, like starting school or a new activity, is what we think of in the field of child development as "positive stress."[2]

What your child wants is not necessarily what they need. Kids rarely voluntarily put themselves in uncomfortable situations. The default is safety. That is what they want—to avoid discomfort at all costs. Most parents know their child's avoidance is unhealthy and limits their experiences and engagement with the larger world. At the same time, it feels uncomfortable and wrong to force your child to do something they don't want to do. The problem is that, when you make the activity a choice, it's unlikely to happen. Avoidance usually wins.

While your big reactor may want to stay in their comfort zone, what they need is exposure. This means creating opportunities for your child to face and work through their discomfort, not enable avoidance. The way kids learn to work through their fears is to live through them and see that they can not only survive but thrive. That's how resilience develops and how sensitive children learn to manage novel or challenging situations with less worry and greater confidence over time. Executing this requires tolerating your child's discomfort, which is no small feat.

For many parents, this discomfort is further complicated by the fact that we are bombarded with messages about the importance of accepting our children for who they are and not projecting our desires—our own hopes and dreams—onto our kids. This is, indeed, very important. You are not supporting your child's true self if they love art and want to do a crafts class, but you want them to be an athlete and sign them up for soccer, an activity they have no interest in.

That said, most parents I work with are not trying to mold their kids in their own image. They are not pushing their kids to do things just to please themselves. They are promoting experiences that they are quite certain their child would enjoy if they could overcome the initial anxiety. Experience from my practice shows that, once these kids have made the transition, they love school or the new designated activity and successfully adapt, à la these recent examples from my practice.

Elliot (five) was refusing to go on a family hike. His parents validated that he was not happy with this plan (even though he loves outdoor adventures) and, as calmly as possible, moved him into the car. Elliot had a blast once on the trail.

Lucy was resisting going to ballet class because her best buddy was not going to be there. Her mom acknowledged that this felt uncomfortable for Lucy but also said attending was a "have-to." Once in the studio, Lucy sulked for a few minutes and then joyfully participated.

When parents trust the process and don't enable the avoidance, even as they are peeling their child off them as they try to exit the car, by and large they return to pick up a smiling child.

And then there is this story from my own annals of parenting. When my son, Sam, was eight, his dad and I had agreed that going to sleepaway camp would be a good experience for him. The two of them went to a dad/son weekend at the camp in the spring and Sam *loved* it. He could not wait to go for the one-month session. But when it came time for drop-off, he panicked and was hysterical, begging us not to leave. It was excruciating for us, but we expected it. I sobbed the entire two hours home but hoped we would hear happy reports within a few days. Alas, all we received were desperate letters from Sam, begging us to come pick him up. One I will never forget included an apology for "this tear-stained page."

Every bone in my body wanted to hop in the car and rescue him. (I was a rescuer—one of my greatest regrets, in hindsight.) But instead, I called the director of the camp to seek an objective assessment. He reported that Sam was very happy and thriving at camp. He was engaged, enjoying the activities, and making friends. But as expected, at rest hour—when the kids are not distracted—they think about home and that's the time the letter writing happens.

This helped me get a grip. I took a step back and asked myself what I would tell another parent in this situation: that Sam could be thriving at camp *and* miss home; that these two truths could coexist. Further, having him stay and work this through would be a tremendous growth experience. Conversely, if we picked him up, we would be sending the message that he was, indeed, not okay without us, and he would be missing an experience that we knew would be fortifying and fulfilling for him.

At the start of week three, the letters took on a different tone. There were no more demands for us to pick him up and he started regaling us with stories of all the adventures and activities he was enjoying. When we arrived to retrieve him at the end of the session, there were sobs once again, but this time they were because he was so sad to leave camp. He begged us to let him stay for the next session. To this day, Sam (now thirty-four), still sees sleepaway camp as one of the most joyful, rewarding, and important growth experiences of his life. My ability to tolerate his distress, and trust the process, enabled him to have this experience. It still stands as one of my proudest moments as a mom.

Difficult feelings are not harmful to children. This is a mindshift that is now quite familiar since it relates to every issue addressed in this book: *feelings—joyful or difficult—are not harmful to children.* Our job is not to rid or protect our children from having difficult emotions (which is actually not possible); rather, it is to help them understand and effectively cope with *all* of their feelings. Shutting down the process is a missed opportunity to help children make sense of, not fear, their feelings.

What kids need when they are distressed is precisely what we need in these moments: someone who listens, accepts our feelings, doesn't judge, and doesn't tell us what to do or try to make it all better; someone who can sit with our uncomfortable feelings and trust that we have the capacity to work them through, with their support.

Labeling and acknowledging difficult feelings helps children understand, gain control over, and work through emotions. Science also shows that validating children's feelings soothes their nervous systems and makes it more likely, although there is no guarantee, that they will become calm.[3]

Cheerleading and coaxing can be paralyzing, not motivating. Having a child who is slow to warm up and hesitant to try new things can be very challenging for parents. It may trigger your own anxiety—especially if you are more extroverted by nature and admire kids who are "go-getters." A common reaction is to act as a cheerleader to convince your child that they can do it. You know that your child would love soccer, but they resist participating, so you regale them with, "But you're great at soccer. You will love the class." You might offer rewards and engage in bribery to motivate your child to participate in the activity: "We will take you for ice cream if you join the group." These tactics can backfire. Trying to cajole kids to participate when they are feeling anxious can make them feel worse and increase their anxiety. It amplifies the shame and self-consciousness they are already experiencing about not being able to do the activity other kids are enjoying. Having attention focused on them, especially when they feel they are being evaluated or judged, can be uncomfortable and exacerbate their stress, as described in the cases in chapter 3.

Also, keep in mind that HSCs are very tuned in to the underlying motives of their parents. They see right through you. They are keenly aware of what you want from them—what will make *you* happy. Looking at it through the lens of logic, you might think that this would motivate your child to want to please you and, thus, take the risk and join in; to show you that they are being "brave" like you want them to be. Instead, the pressure kids experience when they sense how invested you are in their participation and performance can be stifling, not motivating. They have to cope with the risk of disappointing you when they won't jump into the pool to join the class with the other kids, or when they resist joining in the scrum at the playground. This makes it less likely your child will feel confident to take a risk and tackle a new challenge. This is also why I hear from teachers and coaches that kids are almost always more regulated, cooperative, and competent when parents are not present and watching.

It's also why using affirmations can backfire. Having kids repeat mantras that they are strong, brave, and so on, to convince them that they feel this way, can have an empowering effect on some kids. But for many HSCs, having them say these affirmations when they aren't feeling strong or brave or smart in that moment doesn't have the helpful impact you're hoping for. It's a disconnect; it doesn't tune in to or match their internal experience, so they feel more alone—not understood. Further, these highly tuned-in kids pick up on the discomfort their feelings are causing their parents, which can increase their stress.

What's most helpful for these children is to tune in to and show acceptance of their feelings. To wonder with them about why they feel afraid, anxious, or tentative about asserting themselves or trying something new. This makes them feel seen and understood and makes them more likely to see you as someone who can help them look at and reconsider their mindset. This opens the door to a genuine change in their confidence and willingness to try something new.

CASES

Jasper Shirking Swim Lessons

The Presenting Problem

Let's think back to five-year-old Jasper, who refused to go to swim class even though he loves swimming. When Rena and David came to see me, they shared how they had been trying to get Jasper to agree to attend swim class—using all sorts of tactics, none of which have worked. They offered rewards—if he agreed to go, they would take him for a treat afterward. They made threats—they wouldn't be able to take him to the pool that summer if he didn't take lessons, an ultimatum they knew they would never follow through on. They tried to coax him by pointing out all the kids he knows who can swim and how bad he would feel if he still needed to use floaties. To this, Jasper responded, "I hate swimming and don't care if I never learn to swim!" This reaction—kids acting like they don't care about something they really do care about—is a way to ward off feelings of shame because being (negatively) compared is inherently shaming.

One of Jasper's persistent refrains when his parents have tried to coax him to go to swim class has been: "I'll go when I'm six." This is another common reaction to parents trying to get their child to do something that they resist but are fully capable of doing, such as using the "potty" or dressing themselves. The child identifies a definitive point in the future when they'll do what their parents want, which is often a stall tactic, a diversion to get their parents off their back. When parents take their child's "pledge" at face value, they end up disappointed and frustrated when the greatly anticipated date arrives and their child still refuses and keeps moving the goal posts.

I asked Rena and David whether there had been times when Jasper overcame a fear of trying something new. They reported that he was very worried about starting a new school for PK4 and about moving to a new home. These were both "have-tos," not choices, which created opportunities that exposed Jasper to new experiences he ultimately worked through and loved. But Rena and David didn't see swim class as a "have-to"—that is, it wasn't a mandatory activity, in contrast to experiences that have to happen, like changing schools and moving homes. They were out of ideas and felt desperate. They knew participating in a swim class would have multiple benefits for Jasper, but they didn't see a way to convince him to go. They felt paralyzed—unable to make this potentially positive experience happen for their son.

The Analysis

Here is what we know about Jasper that we took into consideration when developing a plan to help him participate in a swim class.

- Jasper is highly sensitive and has always been slow to warm up. Rena and David report that, even as a baby, he showed discomfort in new situations. He was fussier when visiting friends' homes that were unfamiliar compared to those he had been to frequently. It took him a long time to adapt to childcare; he cried every morning for the first month. He ultimately adapted well but went through a similar challenging time when he moved to PK4 at a new school. When they take him to the playground, he always watches for a long time before he starts playing.
- Jasper is self-conscious and doesn't like attention focused on him. He is concerned about how other people see him. He often won't participate in school performances because he doesn't like people looking at him. When his parents praise him for any accomplishment, he doesn't like it and tells them to "stop saying that!"
- Rena and David have focused all their efforts on convincing Jasper to try new things—to get him to change his mind and,

thus, his behavior—something they have no control over. Jasper is a human being. Rena and David can't *make* him agree to go to swim class or to feel less self-conscious. In fact, the more they try to coax him with logic, rewards, and negative consequences, the more fiercely he fights.

- When given the opportunity, Jasper is able to work through the discomfort of trying something new and ultimately takes great pleasure in the experience. We know he loves to swim, so this is not about getting Jasper to do something he has no interest in doing. Learning to swim is also a safety issue—another important factor Rena and David take into consideration.

- Nothing I have learned about Jasper makes me concerned that he *can't* learn to feel comfortable at a swim class. Rena and David agree that this is a situation where they need to set a limit to create the opportunity for Jasper to work through his discomfort by making it a "have-to." The question becomes *how* to make this happen in a way that is loving and supportive and meets Jasper where he is at.

The Plan

Rena and David have a reflective discussion with Jasper. Before they even bring up going to swim class, Rena and David start having conversations with Jasper during moments when he is calm and can be reflective. They talk about what makes him tick: he is a very sensitive, deep thinker who takes time to observe and understand new situations before he feels comfortable joining in. Rena and David acknowledge all the positives about being a "pause to check" kid.

Not only is there nothing wrong with taking time to watch and learn about these new experiences but it is, in fact, a great strategy Jasper has used to get comfortable with and master new things that, now, bring him a lot of joy. For example, when he moved schools, he was more of an observer the first few weeks. Once he understood how the day would go, what the kids and teacher were like, and the kinds of activities they would be doing, he adapted and thrived. They also point out what he may have missed out on if he had not gone to this new school—for example, making a best friend, having access to a much larger playground, and doing all the activities they didn't have at his previous school.

They tell Jasper that going to swim class is a "have-to." Rena and David explain to Jasper that while they know he doesn't want to do a swim class, mommy and daddy have decided that it's a "have-to." Choosing what activities kids do is a mommy/daddy decision. Just as parents choose the school their kids attend to ensure a great education and the foods they eat to ensure healthy and strong growth, parents choose what activities their kids do to help them learn new skills and build strong bodies. Learning to swim is also a "have-to" experience for Jasper because it's about safety. Rena and David are careful to not suggest, in any way, that this activity is open to negotiation; they know that would open up a big, endless, black hole of attempts by Jasper to talk them out of following through on the plan.

When Jasper insists that he won't go and that he'll never get into the pool, they resist the temptation to convince him to like the idea or to tell him what he will and will not do. They listen calmly, validate his discomfort, and reinforce their commitment to support him through it—just as they did when he started a new school and moved to a new home. They refrain from trying to convince him to agree to the plan. They acknowledge that he doesn't like their decision, but they remain clear that they will still be taking him to class. The rest is up to him: he decides how or if he will participate once he is at the pool.

They talk to Jasper about his "worry brain" and "thinking brain." Rena and David explain that there are different parts of our brains. We all have a "worry brain" that focuses on what can go wrong or might be scary. We also have a "thinking brain" that knows we can handle and get past those fears and can help us do so. They use the example of starting a new school. They ask Jasper to list everything that was in his worry brain before he moved to the new school and how his thinking brain helped him overcome his fears.

- He worried the teacher might be mean. Then he went to a get-together at the school in the summer and met the teacher and saw that she was very nice. He recalled she gave him a cupcake and a special name tag with a panda bear on it. His thinking brain was able to assure his worry brain that the teacher was kind. That helped him feel safe in school.

- He worried that they wouldn't have snack time like they did at his old childcare. Then, on the first day, he found out that they have snack time every day.

- He worried about his parents not being allowed to bring him into the school. (The school's policy is that parents drive up and school staff helps kids out of the car and into the classroom.) But after a few days, he saw that it was okay; a kind adult always helped him get to his classroom.

When children look at their fears through the lens of "worry brain" versus "thinking brain," these concerns feel more manageable. It helps children look, with greater objectivity, at their situation and enables them to make sense of and feel more in control of complex feelings.

Rena and David suggest to Jasper that, since he will be going to swim class, it might be a good idea to go through the same "worry" versus "thinking" brain exercise he used for swim class:

- Jasper is afraid the swim teacher will get angry at him if he can't do what she's asking. Thinking brain comes up with the great idea to visit a swim class and be a detective. Jasper can watch to see if the teacher gets mad at the kids who are still learning. Jasper loves the idea of being an investigator.
- Jasper is afraid that he will sink under the water if the teacher doesn't let him wear floaties. He comes up with the idea that, when they visit the class, they can see what the other kids do if they don't have floaties on. He also watches videos that show how kids learn to swim without floaties. And they go to the pool several times before Jasper starts the class so he can see how it feels to be in the water without floaties.

Rena and David connect with the swim teacher in advance. They are mindful of how self-conscious Jasper can be, so they decide it's important to make the teacher aware of this. They explain to her that as counterintuitive as it may seem, it's best not to focus too much attention on him or to coax or cajole him. He experiences it as pressure and may freeze up. They also explain that he doesn't react well to praise. Instead, what works is to narrate what Jasper is doing without any judgment, positive or critical—for example, "You are working really hard to kick your legs. That's helping you float." While this may sound like [helicopter parenting] which has become the catch-all term (slur) for any parent perceived to overprotect their child, the "accommodations" Rena and David request are not enabling Jasper. Quite the opposite. They provide the support their deeply feeling child needs to prevail over a challenging situation that will help him grow. The teacher is open to and appreciative of their input. She wants to do whatever she can to help Jasper feel comfortable to join in.

The Outcome

All of the preparation activities go great. Jasper loves watching videos of kids swimming and visiting a swim class to check it out. Rena brings a pad of paper, which they call their "reporter's notebook," and has Jasper dictate everything he notices about the class: whether the teacher is nice or not, how she keeps the kids safe when they haven't learned to swim yet without floaties, and what exercises they do. Rena thinks they are home free—it's all going swimmingly!

But on the day of Jasper's first class, he announces that he's not going. It all sounded good in theory, when he was just an observer, but when it becomes a reality, he declares he doesn't need swim classes— he knows everything about swimming already by watching the videos and flat-out refuses to go. Rena and David are crestfallen. They dreaded this happening, but they forge ahead and stick to the plan. They acknowledge Jasper's feelings and reiterate that swim classes are a "have-to."

When it's time to get into the car, they tell him that he has two great choices: (1) he can be in charge of his body and get himself into his seat;

(2) if he is unable to do this, they will be his helpers and place him there. He chooses to run away from them. David calmly scoops him up and gets Jasper into the car seat. He refrains from reacting to Jasper's protestations, which include: "You are a terrible daddy; I am taking you back to the daddy store." He also shouts that David is hurting him when his dad is merely holding Jasper firmly in place in order to safely secure him.

When they arrive at the pool, Jasper refuses to join the class in the water. David reminds him that they will be staying for the full forty-five minutes; it's up to Jasper whether he participates or not. When the other kids, two of whom are friends of Jasper's, see that he's not getting into the pool, they are very encouraging, trying to get Jasper to join the group. The more his friends try to woo him, the more uncomfortable Jasper becomes. He starts curling up into a ball and uses baby talk with his dad. David doesn't react to this. He knows that doing so would be shaming to Jasper. David subtly signals to the instructor to remind her that Jasper doesn't like people focusing on and coaxing him because it makes him self-conscious and less likely to feel comfortable to participate. The teacher picks up on this and says to Jasper's friends, "That is so nice that you want Jasper to join. He will do that when he's ready," and redirects their focus to the game they are playing in the pool. Within a few minutes, Jasper has regulated and is watching the class intently.

At this point, David suggests they proceed with their detective work and see what "thinking brain" can tell "worry brain." He takes out his "reporter's notebook" and asks: "Does the teacher [a delightful college student who is warm and funny] get angry at the kids when they can't do the activity/exercise perfectly? Nope, she is very patient, and many of the kids need help. Does she let the kids fall under the water? Nope, none of the kids fall under the water. The teacher makes sure they are always secure."

David asks Jasper what else he notices—are the kids doing anything shown in the videos they watched? Yes, there are many things Jasper can identify. Jasper loves acting like a reporter. He proceeds to color commentate, doing a play-by-play of the action in the pool, and even starts cheering for his friends. But he does not get into the pool during this first session.

When it's time to go to the second session, Jasper doesn't resist going, but he announces in the car that he will not be joining in, he's just going to be a "detective reporter" as he now calls himself. David simply responds: "That's your choice." He doesn't try to convince Jasper to think or feel otherwise.

When they arrive, Jasper immediately sits in the bleachers to watch. The first activity the class does is a game where the kids swim to grab a floating glow stick, which the teacher says they will get to take home if they retrieve it. This is clearly very intriguing to Jasper. Picking up on this, the teacher looks at Jasper and says that she has one for him too, if he changes his mind and wants to play the game. She places the stick on the side of the pool. Jasper looks at David and says, "I don't even like those sticks. I already have so many of them." This kind of defensive response is typical for Jasper when he is torn, which he seems to be in this moment. He clearly wants the stick, but he doesn't want to get into the pool. He resolves this conflict by acting like he couldn't care less about the desired object. As much as David wants to challenge Jasper on this, to point out that he loves glow sticks and getting in the pool would be the right move, he refrains from cajoling and cheerleading and simply says: "That's your choice."

While Jasper doesn't get into the pool at this second session, he does eventually leave the bleachers and sits on the edge of the pool with his feet dangling in the water for the last half of class. When the session is over and the kids are out of the pool, the teacher approaches. She tells Jasper that she has fifteen minutes before her next class and that she will let him do the activity to get the glow stick, if he wants. Jasper loves this idea, and he follows through. Not a surprise that he felt much more comfortable being solo with the teacher and that it got him over the hump of getting into the pool. He easily retrieves the stick and is elated when he gets out.

On the way home, David asks Jasper what they need to put in their reporter's notebook about what "worry brain" had learned that day. Jasper responds that "thinking brain" is so much smarter than "worry brain" and that swimming is easy. Jasper flies into the house when they get home, shows his mom the prized glow stick, and regales her with his amazing feat in the pool.

At this point, all resistance to swim lessons ceases. Further, David and Rena notice an overall increase in Jasper's confidence. He starts doing tasks independently, such as getting dressed in the morning, which he had, to date, insisted he needed help with. As noted in other cases, this is a common phenomenon: when kids master a new skill or situation, they see themselves as more capable and resilient, which positively impacts their overall self-confidence.

The Postscript

Two years later, when Jasper was seven, Rena and David came back to see me. Jasper had become a great and enthusiastic swimmer. He had joined the community swim team which, obviously, is a major development given that competitive activities are very difficult for

Jasper. He is very self-conscious about his performance and doesn't like not being perfect. (More on this in chapter 6.) Jasper had been housebound for three weeks with a bad virus that caused him to miss many practices. When he was finally better and could return to the team, he refused. He was afraid that he would be too far behind the other kids.

Together, we developed a plan similar to the one they implemented when Jasper was just learning to swim. They validated his feelings. They told him that being worried about his performance after a long break made a lot of sense and they would feel the same way. At the same time, they explained that continuing with the team was a commitment and a "have-to." They knew that if they made it a choice, avoidance would prevail, and Jasper would miss out on a very fortifying experience and another chance to muscle through an uncomfortable situation. They also had a great idea to ask the swim coach to do a few private lessons with Jasper to help him regain his confidence. This helped enormously. Jasper was tentative when he initially rejoined the team but rebounded quickly to full participation and a major boost to his self-confidence.

Ella and the Preschool Predicament

The Presenting Problem

A month into the beginning of the school year, I walked into a three-year-old class at one of the preschools where I consult and noticed there was a child, Ella, who was there with her caregiver, Jasmine. While the other kids were playing together in centers, Ella was on her caregiver's lap reading a book for almost all of free play. I asked the lead teacher about why Ella had a caregiver with her at school. She explained that Ella had been having a difficult transition, so her parents had suggested that Ella's caregiver attend with her. This is a very warm and nurturing teacher who felt terrible for Ella and hated to see her distressed, so she had agreed to this plan.

The Analysis

Based on my observation, I was concerned that attending school with a caregiver posed an obstacle to Ella learning to feel safe and comfortable in this setting on her own. All of her attention was on keeping her caregiver close. This meant not engaging directly with any of the children and relying on Jasmine to help her do all the activities instead of building relationships as well as her sense of competence and independence—very important reasons why kids go to school.

It's expected that the transition to preschool, or any big change, will be challenging for children to different degrees based on their temperament. Kids who are more adaptable by nature may jump right in without looking back. Kids who are more sensitive often take longer to feel comfortable in a new, stimulating environment. We expect that HSCs may go through a period of discomfort until they see, within a few days or sometimes weeks, that school is a safe, loving, fun place. Their anxiety eases and they thrive.

With this in mind, I decide to contact Ella's parents, Stephen and Lauren, to collaborate and figure out what the best path forward would be in helping Ella learn to adapt to going to school independently. Stephen and Lauren share that this is Ella's first experience being part of a group and that she has always been slow to warm up to new people and experiences. They have tried to take Ella to a number of different classes, but they always withdraw because she just wants to sit on their laps and won't participate. When they go to the playground or birthday parties, she sticks to them like glue.

Understandably, Stephen and Lauren were very anxious about sending Ella to school. At the same time, they thought that by age three it was important for Ella to be with other kids on a regular basis and to get used to going to school before starting kindergarten. But, when she started crying hysterically every day at drop-off, and wouldn't let them go, they decided it would be best to have her trusted caregiver, Jasmine, stay with her. They thought there was no other way to get her to go to school. They had concluded and accepted that Ella was not capable of feeling comfortable in any group situation on her own. They interpreted her desperate clinging and sobbing at school drop-off as being harmful to her. They didn't see a way to help her adapt without one-on-one support.

I validated their experience. Their worry and consequent solution made a lot of sense. I then shared many stories of my work with children like Ella who are more cautious by nature, but who, with time and support, have made a successful transition to preschool and thrived. Stephen and Lauren agreed that Ella needed the chance to adapt to school on her own and that extricating Jasmine as her helper was a critical next step. In addition, as a practical matter, Jasmine was supposed to be taking care of the new baby; but, because she had to go to preschool three mornings a week with Ella, Lauren had to go through a lot of hoops to change her work schedule so she could care for the baby in Jasmine's absence.

The Plan

They validate Ella's feelings. Stephen and Lauren let her know that they can see how hard it is to separate and go to a completely new place with new people. They don't try to talk her out of her feelings by trying to convince her that she will be fine at school on her own, as tempting as this is. Past experience has taught them that trying to coax and cheerlead Ella to help her overcome difficult feelings backfires. She gets more distressed and puts all of her energy into refuting all of their "talking points."

They remind Ella of past experiences she has had with overcoming a fear of something new. Stephen and Lauren recount the time they went to a cousin's birthday party. Ella was very anxious about it but ended up having a great time after she had a chance to watch for a while and get comfortable.

They share stories about times when they, too, were anxious about starting something new. Stephen talks about how, at a new job he recently started, he was concerned about whether he would be good at it and if he would get along with his new colleagues. But, he explains, the more he did the new job and spent time with the new people he was working with, the less anxious he felt. He also shares how good it felt to make new friends and learn new skills. This serves as a powerful role model and also lets Ella know that she is not alone.

We decide *not* to tell her what the plan will be. This may sound insensitive, but knowing Ella, we believed that telling Ella that Jasmine would no longer go to school with her would cause a lot of anticipatory anxiety. We believed that the best, most sensitive way to help Ella cope with this change was for her to experience it incrementally. This meant having Jasmine take increasingly longer breaks away from the class to create opportunities for Ella to build confidence that she could be okay in her absence.

The Outcome

On day one of the plan, we had Jasmine take a break each hour that Ella was at school. The first was for five minutes, the next was for ten, and the third for fifteen. I was in the classroom and signaled to Jasmine that it was time for her to take a break. Jasmine got down on Ella's eye level and asked her if she could go to the bathroom. (It turns out that Jasmine had *never* left the classroom for fear of distressing Ella.) Ella pleaded for Jasmine not to leave. I interjected: "Jasmine, it's important that you have a chance to go to the bathroom. It's really uncomfortable to hold it in. Ella isn't used to being here without you, but she will be okay. This is a safe, great place." Ella continued to cling to Jasmine, crying and begging her not to go. I gently moved Ella away from Jasmine and signaled for Jasmine to leave. Ella ran to the door and cried, repeating Jasmine's name over and over. The teacher, who had been reading a story, left the group to comfort Ella.

This approach may sound antithetical to being sensitive and responsive. It surely is not something you'll read about on most parenting Instagram accounts. I guided the teacher *not* to abandon the group to focus only on comforting Ella until Jasmine returned. My concern was that this would signal to Ella that a brief separation from Jasmine was too much for her to handle and would set an expectation she would always have an adult to spend one-on-one time with her, which is not sustainable. It would also be an obstacle to experiencing that she could, indeed, manage it. We needed to build her resilience.

Instead, I recommended that the teacher validate that it's hard when Jasmine leaves, give Ella a big hug, and then tell her they would love her to join the group when she's ready. At that point, she should give Ella space and continue with the circle time. I also suggested that the teacher read the book with a lot of animation and participation by the kids. I hoped this might attract Ella's attention. Skeptically, the teacher returned to the group. Ella stayed at the door. But her crying abated as she looked over at the group that was engaged in a silly discussion about the story they were reading. Even in this first separation from Jasmine for five minutes, the sobs became fewer and further between and Ella's attention to the group increased.

We continued with this plan. Each day of that week we increased the periods of separation. By the third week, Jasmine stopped coming altogether. Within a week, Ella stopped crying at drop-off. Within a month, she had become a joyful, full participant in school. Her teacher and parents were ecstatic. They were worried that extricating Jasmine would harm Ella. They were thrilled and relieved to see just how capable and resilient Ella had become. This mindshift led to Ella's parents taking this approach in many other situations with a lot of success.

These types of adaptations don't always happen so quickly. I have worked with children who cling to their parents at drop-off months into the school year, but once the transition is made, they are thriving in the classroom. The process can feel like *Groundhog Day*. Even though parents go through the same routine every day, the transition is still tough. But enabling avoidance is what's harmful to kids. They miss out on so many pleasurable and fortifying experiences, and they miss out on opportunities to see themselves as able to handle and work through the discomfort that we all face as we navigate this world.

SHORT STORIES

Birthday Party Blues

Wendy sought consultation to learn how to help her daughter, Maggie (five), feel comfortable separating from her in social situations, such as visiting a friend's home for a meal or going to the park or a birthday party. Maggie clings to Wendy and won't engage with the other kids. Wendy has come to dread these situations. She sees all the other children happily playing together, having a great time, while Maggie sticks to her like Velcro. This is very agitating and frustrating for Wendy. She tries to coax, cajole, bribe, and sometimes use threats—for example, telling Maggie that she won't have any screen time when they get back home if she just sits in mom's lap at the park; or she can't have any birthday cake if she doesn't join in the activities at the party. These tactics always backfire. They just make Maggie more stressed and resistant. Both mom and Maggie end up feeling awful. On the other hand, Maggie has a very strong but very different relationship with her dad, Justin. She acts much more independently with him. Whereas with Wendy, Maggie is constantly seeking attention for things she is fully capable of doing or figuring out herself. During our consults, we focus on how to scaffold opportunities for Maggie to feel more comfortable not being so dependent on Wendy to be her constant companion and buffer. With a little help from a friend, this leads to the following not-so-tiny victory.

Wendy takes Maggie to the birthday party of one of her closest friends. It's a drop-off event but, as expected, Maggie clings to Wendy and won't let her leave. She insists on sitting on mom's lap. She won't join the festivities. Wendy is frustrated and embarrassed, but she knows that acting on those feelings will not help. She tells Maggie that it's okay to need time to observe before she's ready to join in and that's what they do. After fifteen minutes, Maggie shows no signs of movement. Wendy can feel herself getting increasingly agitated. Every bone in her body wants to leave to end the discomfort, but she remains calm and gives it a little more time. When she is about to break, the mother of the birthday boy approaches and suggests that Wendy leave and have Maggie stay. Wendy is dubious. She also worries that Maggie might experience this as abandonment and that it will harm their relationship, eroding Maggie's trust in her. At a cellular level, it also feels mean to leave Maggie when she is in distress.

At the same time, Wendy knows that if she stays, she's signaling that she doesn't think Maggie can handle it and that she's only safe if mom is present. This will substantially limit Maggie's experiences in the world. It will be a missed opportunity to build her confidence that she is capable on her own. This is something Wendy wants very badly for her daughter and is a primary focus in our consults.

With the support of this other mom, Wendy decides that she needs to take what feels like a very big risk and give Maggie this opportunity to work through the discomfort—to see that she can survive the seemingly unsurvivable. Accordingly, Wendy acknowledges Maggie's fear and hesitance, validates that learning to be at a party without her feels uncomfortable because it is new, and communicates that she has total confidence in her ability to manage it. Then she leaves, even as Maggie is clinging to her and begging her not to go. When Wendy returns ninety minutes later, Maggie is all smiles and begs to stay. The birthday boy's mom reports that Maggie remained upset for a few minutes and then joined in and had a blast.

Jamal Seeking Sameness

It had taken Jamal (four) several weeks to feel comfortable participating in a soccer class last season. Then he thrived. When it comes time to sign up for the next season, Jamal asks if he will have the same coach. When he learns he won't, he refuses to go. His dad, Amari, isn't surprised but doesn't know how to handle it. He has thought about obfuscating: Maybe he shouldn't tell Jamal he will have a new coach to get him to go, but he knows that would be wrong. It would erode Jamal's trust in him. Amari knows that letting Jamal opt out also isn't a good idea. Jamal needs to learn how to accept and adapt to situations like this or he will be missing out on a lot of important experiences. Accordingly, we devise this plan:

- Amari tells Jamal that going to soccer is a "have-to"; that it's a mommy/daddy decision about what activities kids participate in.
- Amari validates Jamal's hesitance; that he loves Coach Scott and wishes he could always be his coach. It's so great that he made such a strong connection with him.
- Amari acknowledges that Jamal doesn't like change but that change happens, and it's his job to help him cope with something new. He reminds Jamal that in the three years he's

been in school, his teachers have changed from year to year and he always ends up loving the new ones once he gets to know them. Amari explains that the same is true for coaches.. They usually change each season. And just like with his teachers, it's likely that Jamal will love this new coach, too.

- Amari contacts the new coach, Patrick, to see if it's possible to arrange a time for Jamal to meet him in advance, which Patrick is happy to do. They meet at a local park for thirty minutes to kick the soccer ball around. Jamal has a great time. As they are parting, Patrick tells Jamal that he's counting on him to do an important job when they meet as a group for the first time: to be in charge of setting up the cones. Jamal is thrilled about this.

As it turns out, on the first day of the new season, Jamal is still hesitant. He says he has a tummy ache. Amari doesn't challenge Jamal on this. He knows that will just result in Jamal becoming more insistent about how ill he is. Instead, even though he's pretty sure Jamal is fine, Amari acknowledges his discomfort and says they're still going to soccer. He assures Jamal that when they arrive, he can decide what's best for him; if he wants to sit and watch because his tummy hurts, that's totally fine. Jamal knows his body best. Amari also ensures that they arrive early so that Jamal can be the first to connect with Patrick.

Jamal complains about his belly and drags his feet as they walk toward where the group will meet. Patrick isn't there yet. When he arrives, Patrick beams at Jamal, hands him the bag of cones, and says, "Jamal! Yes! My cone helper! I'm so glad to see you. Let's get set up." Jamal lights up and enthusiastically gets to work. He is a full participant from this first session on.

FINAL THOUGHTS

As easy as it is to fall into the comparison trap, please take good care of yourself and don't go down that rabbit hole. The go-with-the-flow "dandelions" process these situations very differently than our "orchids." They enter a new classroom, see a giant box of magnetic building blocks they can't wait to play with, and are off to the races. No looking back. Dandelion brains are not wired to process their experiences so deeply. They aren't distracted analyzing everything that's going on around them and, thus, tend to engage more quickly in new activities. The good news is that when we understand the root cause of our HSCs' reactions and provide the opportunity for them to get comfortable in new situations, they often join in and find great joy in participating.

6

Perfectionism, Sore Losing, Low Frustration, and Trouble Tolerating Corrections

Marcel [six] and I were working on writing letters together. When he couldn't make his "O" look exactly like mine, he had a total meltdown. The more I tried to tell him what a good job he was doing, the more agitated he became.

When Serena [five] messes something up, her reaction is very disproportionate. She is incredibly hard on herself. She says she'll never draw again, tears up the paper, and throws herself onto the floor. We try to model how to accept losing and not being perfect, but it doesn't seem to help.

Hayes [seven] is the worst sore loser. We can't play any family games because he goes nuts if he doesn't win. Even though he's great at soccer and makes a lot of goals, the second someone blocks one of his attempts to get the ball into the net he starts screaming that it's unfair and storms off the field. It's embarrassing. I worry about how other kids see him and if they won't want to play with him.

This morning, I very calmly and gently explained to Martin [four] that when he places a cup down on our glass coffee table, he needs to be gentle. His response: "It's not fragile! Don't ever say that to me again! Do you understand? Do you understand!?" This reaction is not atypical—he explodes like this on a regular basis, whenever we need to correct him or set a limit, or when he can't do something perfectly right away. When we try to reason with him, he shuts down. He'll often just cover his ears or run away. We are at a loss as to why he is so hypersensitive and how we are supposed to set limits with him.

I was driving Sari [five] to Hebrew School. I told her that they would probably be learning about Yom Kippur. Sari got revved up and said: "Ergg! Is that the 'I'm sorry' holiday? I don't want to do that holiday!"

These stories encompass a constellation of behaviors that I see frequently in the kids in my practice: perfectionism, sore losing, low frustration, and intolerance to being corrected. They all stem from an intense need to feel in control, coupled with being self-conscious, easily slighted, and quick to feel shamed.

When things don't turn out the way they want or expect, when they don't perform to perfection, it triggers highly sensitive children (HSCs) to feel out of control and experience a strong sense of discomfort, frustration and self-reproach. They don't shake things off the way less intense children do. Just watch any kids' sporting event. One child tries to kick the ball into the goal, misses, and keeps on going, no problem. Another child misses the net, throws herself on the ground, and takes minutes to recover, if she recovers at all. Their perceived failure is intolerable, and they can't cope.

This makes competitive activities especially stressful for these kids. As one child told his dad: "I don't want to play any 'winning' games." Another child refused to go to birthday parties after attending one where they played some games of skill. To cope and protect themselves from the discomfort and shame that gets triggered when they lose, big reactors may try to manipulate the game to win (a.k.a. "cheat") or get angry and quit. I was playing Connect Four with Lucy (five) on a home visit. She made the first move. When it was my turn, I dropped my chip into the slot next to hers—the obvious move. Lucy became agitated and explained, "No, Ms. Claire, I tell you where you can put your pieces."

A related phenomenon is HSCs' outrage at being corrected. They register benign suggestions or directions as personal indictments, not as objective rules you are setting or helpful guidance you are offering. When you ask them not to pull the dog's tail or try to show them how to hold scissors correctly, they experience it as shaming—that they didn't "perform" correctly. They shout things like "Stop telling me that! I already know that!" to shut you down and defend against feeling slighted and incompetent.

Another way HSCs defend against the shame of their perceived failure is to project blame. As adults, we have hopefully learned to cope with and grow from failure. But young children don't yet have that capacity for reflection and impulse control required to effectively cope with failure. They're not saying to themselves: "I hate falling off my scooter. I don't like feeling out of control, and it's embarrassing. But failure is just a part of learning, so I'm going to take my deep breaths and persevere."

To ward off the shame, HSCs engage in all sorts of evasive behavior. Blaming is a biggie. When HSCs lose in a board game, they accuse their opponent of cheating. They miss a goal in soccer and insist their teammate made a bad pass. They fall off their scooter, ten feet from you, and exclaim: "You made my scooter fall!" Or "You bought me a broken scooter!" You try to show them how to balance on it and they shout, "You don't know anything about scooters!"

MINDSHIFTS

It's not my job to solve my child's problems and protect them from all pain. The knee-jerk reaction for many parents is to try to head off the potentially painful situations that provoke their child's perfectionism and sore losing. They stick to activities their child has mastered; they let their child win every game. While completely understandable, these are missed opportunities for the child to learn to accept that developing a new skill is hard work. It involves making a lot of mistakes, and losing is going to happen—it's a part of life—and something we all must learn to deal with. Developing a tolerance for your child's distress in these difficult situations is essential for helping them work through the discomfort.

Cheerleading, coaxing, and affirmations may backfire. Understandably, parents worry about the negative impact that having trouble accepting anything less than perfection, avoiding challenges, giving up easily, and not being able to accept important and necessary corrections will have on their child. A common, reflexive response is to try to talk your child out of their feelings: "That's a great 'O'!"; "But I love your drawing!"; "Nobody's perfect. Just try again"; or "You did such a great job out there even if you didn't make a goal."

The problem is that when children break down in the face of their perceived failure, they are in a highly emotional, irrational state, so trying to use reason or logic to convince your child to snap out of it or change their mind is rarely useful and can backfire—increasing your child's agitation.

HSCs also have superhuman radar for sensing when others are trying to control them, which we are indeed trying to do in these moments—to get them to react differently. This leads to defensiveness and digging their heels in more vehemently. Most importantly, when you jump to reassure, you invalidate your child's experience—as irrational as their reaction may seem. You can't take away your child's feelings. Your job is to help them look at and make sense of their emotions and experiences—a process that can only take place once your child is calm and can think clearly.

While my child may have a hard time being corrected, it's my job to provide guidance and appropriate limits and not to walk on eggshells around them. Many parents end up getting defensive and/or backing off when their child lashes out at them for making a suggestion or setting a limit they don't like. These kinds of reactions can lead to escalation. They are also missed opportunities for kids to learn important lessons about respecting people and possessions. Take Martin, mentioned previously, who slammed the cup on the glass table and flipped out when his mom asked him to be gentler. What Martin needs in that moment is something along the lines of: "I know you don't like it when I give you a direction. It's also my job to help you make good choices. So, you can put your cup down gently or I can't let you bring cups into this room. You decide."

CASES

Camila

The Presenting Problem

Camila (five), described previously, rips up artwork when it's not "perfect," knocks down block structures that are not to her specifications, and quits anything new that she is not expert at immediately, like learning to ride a bike. She has a very low tolerance for any kind of frustration. Her parents, Ashley and Nicole, know this kind of perfectionism isn't healthy for Camila, but they don't know how to help her. They have tried lots of encouragement, affirmations, and rewards (bribes) to get her to keep trying. But these strategies agitate her further. Ashley and Nicole are worried and frustrated at not being able to find a way to help Camila be more resilient and not so hard on herself.

The Analysis

Ashley and Nicole are very focused on raising a strong, self-confident girl by showing her how competent she is. This makes total sense from a logical perspective—that providing a lot of encouragement and praise will help Camila have strong self-esteem and believe in herself. But we think that this approach may be backfiring because Camila is self-conscious and intensely focused on how others see her. She is quick to feel shame when she perceives any type of failure. She picks up on her moms' desire for her to muscle through and experiences it as pressure. She senses their disappointment when she gets frustrated and gives up. The affirmations they offer don't meet her where she's at. She's not feeling brave or strong or proud of her work or accomplishments in those moments, so the affirmations don't resonate and may make her feel worse.

What about her agitation at being offered rewards? We hypothesize it's because Camila wants whatever the "prize" is very badly; but the worry about failure is bigger than the carrot being offered. This puts her in a difficult bind and increases her stress—the opposite of what Camila's moms are trying to instill in her. Like many HSCs, Camila's sixth sense about the underlying meaning and intention of her moms' messages and actions means that praise and rewards are processed as efforts to control her, to make her do things *they want*, which, granted, are all really good for Camila. They want her to feel proud of her work and confident that she can persist to overcome challenges. But her visceral reaction to them trying to change her feelings and behavior, digging her heels in further.

The Plan

Ashley and Nicole's first step is to have a heart-to-heart with Camila to share some important insights and messages. They know that sometimes talking about feelings can be overwhelming for Camila, so they start the conversation by telling her that they've been thinking a lot about how to be the best moms to her. They want to share how they are going to do that. They are clear that she doesn't need to respond unless she wants to share any thoughts or feelings. They are just asking her to listen. I find that, in these discussions, clarifying that you have no expectations of your child takes some of the pressure off and can make them more open to hearing what you have to say.

- First, they share how much they value Camila's strong ideas about things; they know that when something she is creating or doing doesn't come out the way she wants or expects, it's very distressing to her. They give the example of learning to ride a bike. When she couldn't balance right away, it felt really uncomfortable, and she wanted to stop. They totally understand.
- They share stories about times they felt the same way to show her that she is not alone. They incorporate how they learned to accept that failure was part of learning, to send that important message in a safe way through their own experiences. Nicole shares:

> *I loved being on a softball team with my friends. But every time I missed a ball in the outfield or didn't get a hit, I was so overcome with shame that I would walk off the field and refuse to play. My coach helped me see that everyone makes mistakes, and that I was making an important contribution to the team. She also explained that to be part of the team, I couldn't keep walking off the field because it left our team down a player. I had to decide what to do: to quit the team or learn to be okay with not being perfect. I decided to stay on the team because I knew how sad I would be if I wasn't on it. That's how I learned to manage failing. Plus, I had a chance to keep working on my softball skills and got better, even though I was never the best and I still made mistakes. That was the decision that worked for me. You have to decide what's best for you. We can help you think that through if you want.*

Ashley and Nicole stop trying to change Camila's perspective and behavior and learn to tolerate her discomfort. Accordingly, they stop using affirmations, praise, and rewards. When Camila gets frustrated with one of her creations, Ashley and Nicole refrain from cheerleading her and convincing her how great it really is. Instead, they acknowledge that her project didn't turn out the way Camila wanted and show interest in understanding more: What didn't she like about it? Can she think of a way she might keep working on it or does she need a break from it? (They want to be clear they are not pushing an agenda for her to persist.) Is there something they can do to help?

They help Camila "reality test." They watch videos showing famous artists and builders struggling to get things exactly the way they want; that illustrates how working through frustrations and making corrections is an important part of the creative process. This conveys important messages in a safe and entertaining way.

They give back the control to Camila when it comes to learning to ride the two-wheeler. Ashley and Nicole start by telling Camila that they have been encouraging her to keep trying because they know how much she wants to be able to do it. They didn't mean to pressure her and are clear that it's her decision when she wants to try again. They aren't going to bug her about it anymore. They are there to help whenever she's ready.

The Outcome

Changing course has led to Camila getting less easily frustrated and being more persistent. She still sometimes crumples up drawings and erupts when something doesn't go as she wants; but when her moms don't react by coaxing and instead say a simple, "It's frustrating when it doesn't come out the way you want it to," Camila more often than not will try again. When she is not able to persevere, Ashley and Nicole acknowledge that it's a difficult moment and remind Camila that they are there to help her think it through if she'd like. Then they just remain a calm presence to show they love her no matter what and that their love and attention are not connected to her performance.

As for learning to ride the bike, the shift from trying to control Camila to giving her the control results in her announcing, a few days later, that she wants to try again. Ashley and Nicole resist the urge to jump for joy. They now know that this response would likely be processed as pressure and shut Camila down. Instead, they tell her they would be happy to help and ask for her ideas about how they might do that. They make a list of all the things Camila is worried about and how her moms can help her test out and work through those fears. As a result, they come up with a plan that reduces a lot of Camila's anxiety. It includes watching videos of kids learning to ride two-wheelers. This gives Camila two great ideas:

- To practice on her moms' stationary exercise bike to see how it feels to spin the wheels really fast and with the force necessary to stay balanced on a two-wheeler. Camila loves this and does it often.
- To ride alongside a retaining wall in an empty parking lot to give her a safety net if she loses balance.

In less than two weeks, Camila is riding on her own.

Seven-Year-Old Sore at Losing

The Presenting Problem

Max (seven) is playing in a basketball game. His dad, Peter, is in the stands and sees that Max is getting increasingly frustrated that no one is passing him the ball. Just as Peter fears—because Max has a history of sore losing and blaming unfair tactics—he ultimately storms off the court to where Peter is sitting. Max pretends that the reason he left the game is because there is something in his eye; he doesn't want anyone to think he's crying. Then he blurts out to Peter: "It's not fair! No one is passing the ball to me so I can't make any baskets!" With the best of intentions, Peter launches right into encouragement/cheerleading/problem-solving mode: "That happens in games. You can't always get the ball or a basket. What do you think your teammates and coach will think about you walking off? You have to get back out there, buddy."

Max responds: "Stop talking to me right now! You are so annoying!" as he starts to push angrily into Peter. Peter admonishes Max for getting aggressive. This ultimately leads to Max running out of the gym. Peter is feeling distraught about how this behavior will affect Max's continued participation on this team, how his peers see him, and how in the world he is ever going to be able to teach Max how to be more resilient.

The Analysis

Max is a highly sensitive child. He is very self-conscious and focused on how others see his performance. He seeks a lot of praise and needs a lot of external reinforcement.

After we process this incident, Peter is able to see why his response may have backfired; his intended encouragement was not experienced as motivating but, instead, as added stress. Max is tuned in to the fact that Peter is disappointed in him—he wanted Max to buck up and bounce back, which he was not ready or able to do in that moment. This left Max feeling pressured, alone, and misunderstood, making it less likely he would feel confident to get back out there and learn to cope with the challenges of a competitive sport—Peter's ultimate hope for his son.

The Plan

Peter leads with empathy. "Playing team sports can be challenging and frustrating. You don't like it when you don't make baskets or goals, and it makes you want to stop playing." Starting where your child is at maximizes the chance that they will be open to rethinking their perspective, which can ultimately change their reactions.

Peter lets Max know he is not alone in his feelings or with this experience. "It took me a long time to get comfortable with not always being the best on the team and not making the goals and baskets I wanted. I ended up deciding that I would try to manage the frustration and disappointment that can happen in team sports because I didn't want to give up playing those games with my friends."

Peter tells the story of what happened. He recounts the experience matter-of-factly, without judgment, to help Max look at the situation more objectively. "You were open and wanted your teammate to pass the ball to you so you could try for a basket. He kept throwing the ball to other kids, or he went to the basket himself. You really want to make baskets and goals when you play sports. When that doesn't happen, it's very disappointing. Your feelings were so big and overwhelming that you decided not to play anymore."

Peter helps Max think through the natural outcome of his choices. He moves from making statements like, "No one is going to want to play with you" or "You'll never get better at basketball if you keep quitting," as he knows these kinds of responses increase Max's feelings of shame and result in a defensive posture that doesn't help him work through the challenge. Instead, after recounting the story of what happened, Peter asks nonjudgmental questions:

- After you quit the game, what happened? How did you feel?
- How do you think quitting made your coach and teammates feel? Is that how you want them to feel about you?
- Is there a different way you would have liked to respond to this challenging situation? How could you make that happen? How can I help you with that?

This approach—seeking to understand without criticism or judgment—provides an opportunity for children to make connections between their actions and outcomes.

Peter uses his interactions with Max as teachable moments. "I love playing games with you and I know how hard it is when you don't win, or you don't perform the way you want. But it's not fun for me when you accuse me of cheating, change the rules, or attack me. If you're having a hard time, I can help you calm and move on so we can keep playing. If you're not able to do that, we will take a break from the game." He communicates this without frustration and annoyance.

He calmly acknowledges the difficult moment and sets boundaries that he hopes will help Max learn to cope better in these situations. **In the heat of the moment, Peter avoids telling Max what to do.** This always leads to a defensive reaction. Instead, he positions himself as a person who will help Max think through these tricky situations: "Looks like your options are to take some deep breaths and go back into the game or take a break and then figure out how you want to proceed. Which do you think is a better choice for you?"

The Outcome

Now that Peter is no longer trying to change Max's behavior and is giving him the space and opportunity to figure things out for himself, Max is calming more quickly and is sometimes open to engaging in a reflective process to think through these difficult situations. This gives Max the best chance of building resilience. When Peter sets a limit after Max gets revved up and aggressive during a game, Max is now more likely to pull himself together so they can keep playing. All told, this change in approach has solidified a strong bond between Peter and Max, who now feels seen, understood, and respected by his dad.

Olivia Countering Corrections

The Presenting Problem

Olivia (five) is incredibly bright and passionate and extremely sensitive. When her kindergarten teacher teared up at their graduation ceremony, Olivia got up in front of a packed room and gave the teacher a big hug, despite the fact that she typically avoids calling any attention to herself. Her empathy is that big.

Her parents, Anthony and Heather, report that Olivia overreacts to everything. They are especially concerned about her response when they correct or advise her. She accuses them of being mean and descends into self-flagellation. They tell her to pet the dog's body, not pull his tail, and she responds: "You don't think I can do anything right! You're always yelling at me! I am so stupid!" and then pouts. (*Note*: her parents aren't raising their voices in these situations. HSCs often interpret a firm tone of voice as being mean or harsh.) When Anthony and Heather correct Olivia, explaining that the Olympic event they're watching is called "breakdancing," not "hip-hop"—it's the music that's called "hip-hop"—Olivia gets angry and tells them they don't know anything. She shouts that the event is "hip-hop" and runs out of the room.

Then there is an incident at school that finally leads Anthony and Heather to seek consultation. Olivia is sobbing at school pick-up. Through her tears, she tells Heather that the teacher didn't give her a goodie bag. This doesn't sound right to Heather. She reaches out to the teacher who explains that Olivia and a friend were being very loud and disruptive to peers who were playing in the block area, so she directed them to move to the quiet corner to take a break. The other child had no problem with this. Oliva, on the other hand, had a major meltdown. The school day ended soon thereafter. At their goodbye circle, the teacher was handing out goodie bags from a special event they had that day. Olivia was still so distressed that she didn't accept her bag. She just ran out of the classroom.

Anthony and Heather are troubled by Olivia's negative statements about herself and her total intolerance of being mistaken about anything. They are especially concerned about her lying. They feel like their hands are tied: Isn't it their job to guide her when she is doing something unacceptable or when she is wrong?

The Analysis

We believe the root of this behavior is that Olivia is quick to feel shame. Anthony and Heather see this show up in many ways. When Olivia makes a mistake or can't do something perfectly, she blames them or makes up excuses for why it happened and wasn't her fault. Given this mindset, it makes sense given this mindset that she might also experience correction as criticism, get angry at the messenger, and refute any suggestion that she is incorrect or doing something wrong.

What about the negative self-talk? Anthony and Heather suspect that it is, in part, a reflection of her tendency to judge herself harshly. She is a perfectionist. They also think that she knows these statements are very triggering to them and will get them to back off.

And the lying? I explain to Anthony and Heather that when five-year-olds tell untruths, it's not considered lying in the moral or ethical sense; children this age don't fully understand the distinction between truth and fiction. Lying, in this case, is a coping mechanism—to avoid the discomfort of owning what actually happened that felt so shaming. Olivia recounts *her experience*—she didn't get a goodie bag. Of course, an "instant replay" would show that the teacher had, in fact, offered Olivia a goodie bag, which she *chose* not to accept. But this is not how Olivia processed the event. It is not her truth. If her mom had reprimanded Olivia for lying, it's likely her shame would have escalated, overwhelming her further, with no productive outcome.

Heather and Anthony also clearly see the powerful role of temperament in understanding Olivia's behavior. Her peer, who experienced the exact same correction from the teacher, had a completely different reaction because he didn't process it in this personal way. That enabled him to accept and follow the direction. Olivia, on the other hand, was mortified and so deeply affected that she couldn't cope in an effective way.

The Plan

Tuning in and connecting. In a quiet moment, Anthony and Heather have a reflective conversation with Olivia to show compassion and understanding and to help her gain self-awareness about how her feelings affect her actions. They share the following key messages:

- **They start by acknowledging** Olivia's strong need to feel in control and be "right" about everything. They recount several examples of how these attributes have led to positive outcomes. She wanted to be the first to ride a two-wheeler, so she tried and tried until she got it. She reads books over and over so she can recall the stories to share with friends and family.

  They also acknowledge that it's really hard for her when she doesn't get something right. It feels very uncomfortable to be corrected. It makes her feel bad about herself. They totally understand. At the same time, they note that nobody ever gets everything right. They share their own stories of how accepting guidance helped them master new skills and make good choices. They ask Olivia to tell stories of when she has seen her teachers correct her classmates and guide them to make better decisions. They normalize that everyone needs help; Olivia is not being singled out, and that being offered help doesn't mean people think less of her.

- **They tell Olivia that it's the job of the adults who care for her to guide her—to keep her safe and teach her to make good choices.** They give her concrete examples, like when they have to guide her not to pull the dog's tail. They do this because they love her—they don't want the dog to pounce on her or to not want to cuddle with her, which they know would make Olivia feel bad. So, even though she may not like it, they are still going to be her guides, which might mean separating her from the dog if she is not able to follow the rules.

Responding to the negative self-talk. When Olivia says things like, "I'm an idiot. You think I'm dumb and wish I wasn't in this family" when she is being corrected, Anthony and Heather now respond with compassion. They no longer try to talk her out of her feelings. Instead, they start with validation: "I know you don't like it when we have to help you make a different choice. We're glad you can tell us exactly how you feel, and we want you to know what we're thinking and feeling. We think you are incredibly smart and that you are also still learning about how to make good choices; that's what smart people do, they keep learning. Even mommy and daddy are still learning." Then they move on with implementing whatever correction has to be made; for example, "I can't let you pull Maggie's tail. You have two great choices: (1) I can get you something safe to pull instead of Maggie's tail and then you can stay in the same room with her; or (2) if you choose to keep pulling her tail, you can play in a room away from Maggie—you decide." (For more on how to deal with negative self-talk, see chapter 8.)

Dealing with Olivia's demands that she is always right. Anthony and Heather recognize that trying to get Olivia to accept that she is wrong about something is a useless endeavor. She just doubles down to defend her position. Now when she insists on a falsehood—the event is called hip-hop or dinosaurs still roam the earth—they simply respond that they have different information and offer to be detectives together to go onto the internet and see what they can learn. They also role model. Anthony purposefully says something false, like carrots grow on trees. Heather chimes in and says she thought they grew in the ground. Together they go online to find the correct answer. When they do, Anthony declares: "Wow—thanks for helping me get it right."

Addressing the "lie." Anthony and Heather tell Olivia that together with her teacher, Ms. Salazar, they are "Team Olivia." They communicate so they can work together to help her be her best Olivia. (This is the messaging I suggest parents use to explain why parents and teachers talk; not to get kids in trouble but, rather, to collaborate to support them. Otherwise, kids feel like all the adults in their world are talking about them, evaluating and ganging up on them, and getting them into trouble.) They explain that they spoke to Ms. Salazar to understand what had made the day so difficult for Olivia and now they don't understand. They don't accuse her of lying or even address the untruth head on. Instead, they speak to the underlying challenge that led to the behavior. They show empathy for how hard it is for Olivia when she is corrected. They know that she was so upset that she wasn't able to accept the goodie bag. That must have been very disappointing. They also remind

Olivia that corrections will happen—that is the job of the adults who care for her and want to help her learn to make good choices.

Retelling the story accurately, with understanding and compassion, is a gentle and effective way to "set the record straight"—to teach the important lesson they want to communicate to Olivia without triggering her shame or defensiveness. They hope this will make it more likely she will feel safe and comfortable telling the truth.

The Outcome

This change in approach results in some big, positive developments:

- There is a significant reduction in negative self-talk. Anthony and Heather are very relieved about this; they are hopeful that Olivia may not be internalizing corrections as shaming.

- Olivia is less reactive to corrections as an indictment of her personhood, but there are still times when she deflects or melts down. Anthony and Heather are now comfortable tolerating her discomfort and giving her space to work it through. They resist defending themselves when she blames them, which has resulted in Olivia doing a lot less blaming.

- Olivia now often asks her parents to tell stories of when they made mistakes and had to be corrected. They know this means she is trying to make sense of her own feelings and experiences, which is a good thing.

- Olivia is increasingly open to investigating to learn new information and is often better able to tolerate when she is incorrect. She has taken to saying, "Nobody's always right!"

SHORT STORIES

When Your Child Laughs or Is Otherwise Evasive When Corrected

Think back to Martin, who flipped out when his mom, Samantha, asked him to be more careful when putting his cup on the glass table. She had been reacting to his overreactions with outrage. This wasn't resulting in any positive changes; Martin just escalated. The following shift in approach helped:

- **Samantha ignores Martin's evasive behavior: laughing, sticking out his tongue, and covering his ears.** She doesn't even force him to make eye contact as that results in yet another power struggle since she can't actually make him look at her when she's talking. It also diverts attention from the incident at hand. She now just hugs him closely, if he'll let her, and says: "I know, you don't like when mommy needs to help you make a good choice."

- **She discusses the incident when Martin is calm.** Samantha knows that when Martin is overwhelmed, he doesn't have access to the part of his brain that enables him to think and reason. She waits until he is calm to engage in any reflecting and teaching. She starts by retelling the story of what happened: "Mommy asked you to be gentle when you put your cup down on the glass table because it's fragile and can break. I meant this to be helpful—just like when your teachers give you a direction at school—but you got very upset." Samantha acknowledges that he might hear her direction as harsh or angry, because he doesn't like to be corrected, but that the tone she is using is just clear and firm. She is not angry. Because she loves him, she is helping him make good choices.

- **Samantha asks for permission to give guidance before launching in with her ideas.** "I see you are working hard to make the scissors work. It can take practice to use scissors. I have some ideas for how to help. Let me know if you'd like to hear them." For kids who have a hard time taking direction, this approach can be a game changer. It makes them much more open to hearing about and acting on your ideas.

- **She follows through with important limits and tolerates Martin's upset.** "I know you don't like it when I give you a direction, but that's my job. Your two great choices are (1) to use the truck safely or (2) to keep banging it too hard on the floor, in which case the truck will have to take a toy time-out. You decide."

Approaching these incidents in this new way has resulted in Martin being less defensive and evasive. It has also made Samantha less on edge; she's no longer walking on eggshells around Martin now that she has a plan for how to respond and stay in charge in a loving way in these situations. This has made for a more loving connection between them, overall.

When Your Child Feels Ashamed and Lashes Out

Tommy explains:

> Zoe [seven] and some friends were making beaded bracelets in our backyard. Zoe's bracelet fell to the ground and came apart. One

of her friends immediately started to help to retrieve the beads. Zoe started shouting at her and told her she should go home. I was totally mortified. I told Zoe she couldn't treat her friend that way and insisted she apologize. She refused, so I told the friend I was sorry for Zoe's behavior. Zoe then ran into the house and slammed the door. When her mom and I tried to talk to her about the incident later that day, she covered her ears and told us to go away. How are we supposed to help her with this very disturbing, unkind behavior?

This is a reaction I see frequently with my HSCs that I believe is triggered by the two key factors you have seen at play for many of the kids featured in this book: (1) they have a very strong need to feel in control—they hate the unexpected, when things don't happen the way they want; and, (2) they are self-conscious and quick to feel ashamed. They experience any "mistake" or accident as a blight on their character or ability. Zoe's reaction to her friend's assistance likely increased her shame; needing help is processed as weakness.

What about Zoe's refusal to discuss the incident or to apologize? It's not for lack of empathy; Zoe is a very empathetic and compassionate child. We believe her resistance to saying "sorry" is because it means acknowledging that she acted hurtfully. She feels a lot of shame about this, which is compounded by her dad's anger at her behavior. When Tommy apologizes for her, it intensifies her shame. (Imagine you are in a restaurant and get snippy with the waiter. The person you're with says to the waiter, "I apologize for my partner's behavior.") Zoe's only coping mechanism at this point is to extricate herself from this overwhelming situation.

Making the following course corrections helps:

- Her parents, Tommy and Megan, acknowledge that it feels uncomfortable when something goes wrong—that is, when Zoe makes a mistake or perceives she has failed in some way. When someone tries to help, it can make it feel worse.
- They stop apologizing for Zoe. And they don't try to force her to say "sorry" for two important reasons: (1) it falls into the category of things they can't make her do, so it just leads to a protracted power struggle when she resists saying a mea culpa; and (2) it would be devoid of meaning. Instead, Tommy and Megan acknowledge that saying "sorry" feels hard because it means accepting that she has done something hurtful. Lots of people have a difficult time saying "sorry." She's a really good kid who had a difficult moment and acted out—that happens. We all say and do things we don't mean when we are in an upset state.

  They explain that there are lots of different ways to apologize, other than looking someone in the eye and saying "sorry." She can use American Sign Language for "I'm sorry" by making a fist and rubbing/circling it over her heart. (This brilliant idea came from a mom who shared that she learned it from seeing Carmy use it on an episode of *The Bear*, and it was working great for her daughter—and her husband!) She can write/dictate a note, draw a picture, offer a hug, or send a voice memo (with mom and dad's help). When Zoe still can't/won't apologize or take responsibility in any form, they share: "I feel much better when I apologize. It's a relief. But you are your own person and need to decide. Let me know if you change your mind and how I can help." Not forcing it (which is just fodder for a fight) and giving kids space makes it more likely they will ultimately decide to apologize on their own.

Tommy and Megan are finding that this new approach has resulted in Zoe lashing out less frequently and intensely in similar situations. She is also getting better at saying "sorry" using the strategies they suggested.

FINAL THOUGHTS

You can see how HSCs' intense need for control and being quick to feel ashamed is at the epicenter of many challenges they face—perfectionism, low tolerance for frustration, and difficulty being corrected are no exceptions. It's also why typical parenting strategies tend not to work with these kids, and why it's so important to take the time to figure out the root cause of their behavior. Once you understand the underlying thoughts and feelings that are driving your child's actions, you have the insight necessary to make course corrections as illustrated in the stories in this chapter and entire book.

7

Relationship Challenges with Siblings and Peers

It turns out our little Miranda [five] is a "mean girl." Her teacher reports that she is very bossy at school. She dictates what her peers can and cannot do. She uses threats to get her way. She tells kids they won't be invited to her house for a playdate if they don't do what she wants. She excludes others, especially when she is one-on-one with another child. She tells the "intruder" to go away, repeating that perennial preschool mantra: "No thank you!" She also criticizes her classmates' work and teases them when they make mistakes. At home, she constantly puts her brother down and won't let him play with her unless he follows all her commands. He can't have a say in anything. We are horrified by this behavior and have no idea where it comes from. We are constantly talking about kindness in our home, and her school focuses a lot on social-emotional development and learning. We can't figure out how to get her to be the kind person we want her to be. It feels terrible as a parent to not like your child.

These kinds of social dynamics are typical for families who come to see me. Not surprisingly, research shows that highly sensitive children (HSCs) experience more challenges in their social relationships than less sensitive children, due to their heightened emotional responsiveness, sensitivity to environmental stimuli, and deep processing of information.[1] Specifically:

HSCs have an intense need to be in control. This makes group situations inherently challenging as there is so much out of kids' control. To cope, HSCs may try to dictate what others can and can't do to ensure that things go the way they want. Like Serena (four), who always has to be in charge: she assigns all the roles when playing pretend with peers; she decides whether the block structure will be for dinosaurs or superheroes. She dictates where classmates sit at the snack table. If her peers don't comply, she stomps off and refuses to play or makes threats that she will tell the teacher on them or not invite them to her birthday party. This stance makes getting along in a group or on a team challenging.

HSCs tend to overanalyze. As a result, they can be more self-conscious, experience more self-doubt and insecurity, and worry more about social approval or rejection. They often misinterpret the meaning of others' actions. They may feel hurt when another child is simply choosing to engage in a different activity or opts to sit next to another child at snack time. This makes social situations stressful for highly sensitive children. It also results in lashing out at their peers when they perceive rejection or insult, which can negatively affect their relationships.

HSCs have trouble with competition. As discussed at length in chapter 6, HSCs have a difficult time not being first or the winner. It triggers feelings of self-doubt and shame. When they aren't the "best," they experience it as failure. This makes any kind of game play quite challenging for big reactors. They make accusations of unfairness, try to change the rules, and melt down or quit when they sense defeat. They demand to be first in all situations. One child insisted her parents take her to school a full forty-five minutes before the doors open to ensure her place at the front of the line.

Big reactors may also project their feelings of vulnerability onto others. For example, Sumi makes fun of peers when they give an incorrect answer during circle time or miss getting the ball into the basket. She can't tolerate any feelings of weakness or failure in herself. She has a strong need to be number one and the most skilled at everything. Her own feelings of vulnerability are triggered when she sees other kids stumbling. She projects these difficult emotions onto others by teasing.

This need to be the best can also lead to bragging and sometimes telling untruths to gain stature. HSCs sometimes feel they have to outdo everyone to compensate for feelings of insecurity. When a peer or sibling shares a fact, for example, about the planets, they might respond: "I already know that!" At circle time, when a peer shares something special, such as having gone on a trip to Disney World, they respond: "I've been to Disney World one hundred times!" When a child shares that they learned to ride a big kid bike, the HSC responds: "I learned to ride a bike when I was two!"

HSCs tend to prefer small groups or one-on-one interactions. The intensity and complexity of the group dynamic can feel overwhelming for big reactors, both emotionally and from a sensory perspective. To cope, they might withdraw and resist engaging in play with peers. Or they might get revved up and dysregulated, making it hard for them to engage in calm, connected collaboration with other children.

Excluding peers is another coping mechanism for children who feel uncomfortable with group dynamics. They may prefer to play with only one child and shun others who try to join. Or they might dictate who can and can't participate to maintain control and ensure they won't be left behind. For example, Mica (six), who, in his pod during COVID, insisted they create "teams" that would do everything together to guarantee he had at least one child in his corner, indemnifying himself from being left out.

Children might also exclude others to gain a sense of power, to feel like they are the boss. This behavior sometimes emerges when there is a new baby in the family. The older child senses a loss of power and starts bossing people around to regain the stature they perceive is at risk. It also happens when a child has older siblings who boss them around—they displace their need for power in interactions with others.

HSCs can also be deeply empathetic, thoughtful, and capable of forming very positive, meaningful relationships. These two realities can coexist. HSCs might develop a strong connection with some peers and struggle with others—often based on the "fit" and the characteristics of the situation at hand. Their shifts in mood can also be a factor: one minute they show deep compassion and the next they are unkind.

The social challenges some HSCs encounter can be quite complex. In this chapter, I focus on an approach to helping parents guide their children through tough situations that has resulted in more social success. There are times, however, when additional support services are necessary. For example, schools need to intervene when a child is being systematically excluded, ganged up on, or targeted in harmful ways. Programs like lunch bunches and social skills groups can be very helpful for kids who are having a hard time engaging in healthy socialization at school. Private counseling may be necessary to help a child work through social anxiety or self-esteem and self-confidence issues that underlie their challenges. Seeking help is important if your child's social struggles are pervasive and interfering in their daily functioning and the development of their sense of self—regardless of whether your child is the victim or the aggressor.

Note that I intentionally refrain from using the word "bully"—a term that currently is being attributed to kids as young as three. Bullies, as Michelle Obama puts it best, are "scared people acting scary."[2] They don't start out wanting to be mean and harmful. They are acting on their own feelings of self-doubt and insecurity. Labeling them bullies is stigmatizing. It reinforces their negative self-concept and the underlying fears and anxieties that are at the root of their unkind behavior. Shaming them in this way makes any kind of meaningful change impossible. These kids need limits and boundaries implemented with empathy about how challenging it is to manage their strong, complex emotions.

MINDSHIFTS

Guiding parents to find effective ways to help their children with some of these complex social challenges always starts with some key mindshifts.

My child is not acting mean on purpose when they boss other kids around, say hurtful things, exclude peers, and act in other unkind ways. They are struggling with difficult feelings of insecurity, self-doubt, and anxiety. They need our help, and maybe professional help, to explore and work through these feelings and experiences in more positive ways.

Teaching about kindness is often not enough. It's certainly important to talk about kindness as an important value in your family and to model it. But for kids who act unkind due to their own insecurities and self-doubt, or because of their intense need to be in control, encouraging kids to be kind is often insufficient to bring about change. The underlying issues that drive the unkind behavior need to be addressed. Kids three and older "know" what's right and wrong. They will tell you straight up that leaving kids out or saying mean things is not okay. But in the moment, when they are triggered, their reactive brain takes over; their emotions and impulses prevail.

My child needs my support, not my criticism or judgment. You love your child so much that it's distressing to see them behave in ways you fear won't bode well for them. This propels most parents into reactive mode, which often takes the form of schooling—trying to convince the child to change their ways: "Why would your friends want to play if you won't share?"; or "We can't do playdates if you're going to boss your friends around. They don't like it." While you mean to be helpful, these kinds of responses are experienced as criticism and shaming, which launches your child into defensive, self-protective, and reactive-brain mode. This prevents any possibility for reflection and behavior change—the ultimate goal.

My job is not to tell my child what to do. This is often the most difficult shift to make because the nature of parenting is to do whatever we can to protect our children from painful situations.

We think that if we can just get our important (brilliant! insightful!) points across, our kids will change their behavior and all will be right with the world.

But as human nature would have it, the knee-jerk, self-preservation reaction to being told what to do is to get defensive. Kids are no exception, especially those who are all about power. Trying to control their behavior by giving advice rarely has the impact you hope for. Most big reactors simply shut you down. Not to mention that you can't solve these problems for your child. You are not in the classroom, on the playground, or on a playdate to intervene or rescue them. They need the insight and tools to manage these situations on their own. Our job is to engage with and respond to our kids in a way that opens them up to reflecting on difficult encounters and considering alternative, more positive and productive ways to respond to and engage with their peers. You do this by being the person they can trust to help them think through their experiences without criticism or judgment—to provide opportunities to reflect on and decide for themselves what, if any, changes they want to make to their behavior. This is the kind of response most of us are hoping for when we go to friends or family with a problem. We don't want them to tell us what to do, which feels patronizing and dismissive. We want someone who, without judgment, helps us look at the situation from 360 degrees so we can think through what course corrections we might want to make.

I need to manage my own reactions. When you get revved up and reactive in these triggering moments, it can further overwhelm your child and be an obstacle to helping them get calm and clear. They are already dealing with their own big, uncomfortable feelings. Sensing our disappointment and worry about their behavior compounds their distress and makes it much less likely they will be able to work through the challenge they are facing in a positive way.

CASES

Caleb and the Playground Problem

The Presenting Problem

Mira and Greg are concerned about how their son, Caleb (five), interacts with his peers. He often annoys the other children to get their attention. Recently at the playground, he was trying to enter a game of tag with some of the neighborhood kids. He randomly tagged them, not following the rules. His peers were clearly getting annoyed. They kept telling him to stop. Caleb ignored their pleas and just got sillier. He started to make fun of their names, calling Isaac "Pisak," and Owen "Bowen." At this point, the kids told him to go away. Caleb ran to Mira, who had been sitting on a bench observing. He was angry and crying because the kids were being mean to him and not letting him play.

Mira tried to teach him a lesson: "What do you expect? Why would kids want to play with you when you're not playing by the rules and are making fun of their names? And then you don't stop when they ask you to. They don't like it, so of course they don't want to play with you." Caleb got more upset and told Mira she's being mean. He accused her of taking the other kids' side, that she doesn't know anything, she doesn't understand, and she never listens to him.

Mira and Greg feel awful. They clearly see that the way Caleb is acting with other kids is resulting in rejection, which is having a very negative effect on him and is painful for them to witness. They feel sad for Caleb. At the same time, they are frustrated and at a loss as to how to help him see that *his* behavior is causing the problem and the solution is in *his* hands; he would have more positive social interactions and feel better about himself if he played more appropriately. But he gets defensive the second they try to talk to him about it. He acts like he is the victim and projects all the blame onto the other kids. Mira and Greg are despairing over how to help him.

The Analysis

I do a deep dive into what makes Caleb tick. I learn that he is an HSC who is easily slighted. He misinterprets typical social situations. He thinks it's an insult when he is not chosen to be "It" first, or when a friend tries to show him how to play a game. He also has a hard time figuring out how to join group interactions. He does great when he has one-on-one playdates, but he is less certain of himself on the playground. His gross motor skills are not his strength, so he feels intimidated by other kids who are very agile. He is overwhelmed by big-group dynamics, which results in dysregulation. Sometimes he just withdraws and plays on his own. This factor exacerbates the problem because it limits Caleb's opportunities to learn the rules of engagement with a group. When he does decide to join in, his anxiety causes him to get overexcitable and silly—behavior that is often a signal of discomfort. During school conferences, Caleb's teacher reports that, at recess, he plays with one preferred child. Caleb plays on his own if that child is not at school or is otherwise engaged.

After assessing the situation, we suspect that Mira and Greg's efforts to help Caleb in these situations is backfiring because:

- He experiences the "schooling" as criticism and interprets it as his parents siding with the other children. This results in Caleb getting defensive and doesn't position Mira and Greg to be the helpers he needs them to be.

- Since Caleb can be demand avoidant, telling him what to do—how to correct his behavior—makes him dig in his heels and not consider himself to other ways of interacting.

The Plan

They start with empathy, not shame. Mira and Greg avoid schooling and criticizing and, instead, lead with empathy. "I can see how disappointed and sad you are that the kids don't want you to play." This shows Caleb that he is seen and that they are on his side. Validation and empathy make children feel understood and not alone, opening them up and making it more likely they will feel safe to reflect on difficult situations and feelings, which is the first and most crucial step for making behavioral changes. This doesn't mean agreeing with Caleb's actions. It means showing him they understand and are tuned in to his experience.

They resist telling Caleb what to do and empower him to be his own best problem-solver. Now, when Caleb comes to them complaining about a social challenge, they respond: "I can see this is a tough situation. You're not happy with how things are going. Do you want help thinking it through?" If he's not ready to engage in this process, in a neutral tone, without judgment, they say: "I guess you have two options: you can decide to play according to the rules, call kids by their real names, and be accepted by the group; or, you can keep playing by your own rules, make fun of their names, and risk rejection. Which choice do you think is better for you?" Presenting it this way clearly communicates to Caleb that they are not trying to control him. How he reacts is completely up to him, which, in fact, it is.

Mira and Greg normalize that learning to get along with friends can take some time and practice. They suggest being social detectives[3] together to figure out what works to make good friends. They start by retelling the story of what happened, matter-of-factly, without any criticism, judgment, or editorial commentary: "You wanted to play tag with the kids at the park. You started to tag them even though you weren't 'It.' They didn't like that and asked you to stop. You chose to keep doing it. Then you started making fun of their names. The kids said you couldn't play. Now let's put on our social detective hats and see if we can figure this out together." They ask questions to help Caleb analyze the situation: "What did you want to happen when you joined their game?"; "Did it work out as you expected?"; "How do you think tagging kids when you weren't 'It' made them feel?"; "How do you think that affected their reaction to you?"; "Did the outcome make you happy? Sad? Disappointed?"; and "Is there anything you want to do differently next time?"

Asking questions versus "correcting" reduces defensiveness and provides an opportunity for children to make connections between their actions and outcomes. This makes it more likely they will ultimately change their behavior. At the end of the day, your children need to learn to solve their own problems. When you take over, you send the message that you are responsible for the solutions. It's also a missed opportunity to show your child that you have confidence that they can figure it out.

They provide a tool to help Caleb make course corrections in the moment. Mira and Greg come up with a cue word that they will say out loud when they see Caleb going down a path that may lead to problems. This will help him pause and make a course correction before things spiral out of control. Caleb chooses "gobbledygook." Using a cue word is a gentle, non-shaming way to show your child that you are on their side and their helper and that you see what's going on and are supporting them in making positive course corrections. It's also a great tool for teaching self-regulation.

They *don't* warn Caleb in advance about misbehaving. You may think (hope) that reminding your child not to hit, push, throw, bite, or be unkind before they enter a group setting will prevent this behavior. Or that making threats will motivate them to do better: "If Ms. Jackson tells me you hit your friends today, there will be no screen time." These warnings often increase the likelihood children will act out, as they send the message that they are *trouble* and that you are anticipating that they will behave badly. The child internalizes this message. It becomes part of their self-narrative and they act on it.

They role-play how to join group situations. Greg and Mira engage Caleb in acting out different social scenarios, including reenacting the situation on the playground when he was rejected. Caleb plays himself but also takes on the role of the other kids so he can see how it feels from their perspective. When Greg or Mira plays the role of Caleb, it gives them a chance to model effective options, which serves as a powerful teaching tool.

They plan playdates to provide practice. They get recommendations from his teacher about kids she thinks would be a good fit for him to engage with outside of school. They also try to arrange some group playdates at local parks to give Caleb a chance to practice the rules of engagement for group games that will hopefully help him on the school playground.

I connect with Caleb's teacher to learn more about what she is observing and how we might collaborate. We discuss ways the teacher can help Caleb feel more comfortable in unstructured group activities. The teacher agrees to partner Caleb up with kids she thinks would be a good match and has them engage in tasks together to expand his friend universe beyond his one preferred pal. She will slowly increase the size of these small groups. I suggest that she come up with a cue word with Caleb that they can use at school to compliment what they are doing at home. We talk with the school counselor about having Caleb do a lunch bunch/social skills group, and we connect with the aides on the playground about helping Caleb get involved in some of the group games with support.

The Outcome

Most importantly, taking all of these steps has greatly reduced the stress between Caleb and his parents and has forged a stronger bond between them. He sees them as his helpers and is much less defensive.

The playdates go well when there are two kids. When they add a third child to the mix, it doesn't go so well because Caleb wants to monopolize one child and the other is left out. Or Caleb is excluded and that's a nightmare. They hope to build up to the point when they can do playdates with multiple kids, but for now, they are sticking with having one child over to their home at a time. This also makes it more manageable for Mira and Greg to step in to help Caleb think through tricky situations. Three is too complicated.

Using the cue word sometimes works and sometimes doesn't. When it does, Caleb is able to change his approach with very positive outcomes, especially on the playground. There has been no more teasing. When saying the cue word doesn't help Caleb switch gears, they give him a break without shaming him. If he wants to process the incident to see if he can move on and rejoin his playmate or the group, depending on the situation, they do that. If he's not open to a reflective discussion in the moment, they sit quietly with him until he's ready to move on.

To further support Caleb, Mira and Greg decide to have him do a round of occupational therapy to work on some core muscle strength and coordination and to build his resilience and self-confidence. This is having a hugely positive impact on Caleb, especially on the playground where he feels a greater sense of competence.

The school reports that they also see positive changes as a result of the interventions. Caleb plays more with the kids he has playdates with outside of school. He has more success playing some of the group games. The role-playing Mira and Greg have engaged him in has helped a lot with understanding the rules of engagement in group play.

Sasha Being Bossy

The Presenting Problem

Sasha (six) is controlling and bossy in her play with peers. Her parents, Kathryn and Kevin, dread playdates because the visiting child always ends up in tears or is annoyed with Sasha and asks to leave. They have been responding by getting upset with Sasha, warning: "No one will want to play with you if you are always bossing them around." Or "Look at how sad your friend is. She wants to go home. Is that what you want? You'll have to play by yourself and there will be no screens all afternoon." Historically, this has led to epic screaming matches between them, resulting in everyone feeling miserable and no positive changes. When Kathryn or Kevin tries to talk to Sasha about it, she covers her ears and shuts the conversation down. They are very concerned about this "mean" behavior, how it's affecting her friendships, and what they can do about it.

As for school, her teachers from last year reported that Sasha was bossy and that her peers gave in to her demands. Now in kindergarten, most of the kids don't tolerate it. They just reject her. Her current teachers report that Sasha had connected with one peer, Reagan, who is more passive and let Sasha be in charge. Sasha became very possessive of Reagan. But after a month or so, Reagan started to play more with another classmate. Since then, Sasha has been mean to Reagan, causing significant problems. The teacher also recently reported that Sasha has been making up stories, telling untruths: she has two horses and her family owns a castle!

The Analysis

Kathryn and Kevin describe Sasha as a very intense, sensitive child with high EQ (emotional quotient/intelligence). She is keenly tuned in to social dynamics and is hyper-focused on how other kids see her. She needs to be in control and in charge and is easily slighted. They have a hard time setting limits with her at home. They hate the battles and often give in to Sasha's demands. She is an only child, so she hasn't had a lot of experience to learn and share.

As often happens in families with a single child and very loving parents, the world pretty much revolves around Sasha. She hasn't had a lot of experience learning to be flexible and collaborative. These are skills that can be particularly challenging for kids who are highly sensitive and require a lot of practice to build. Sasha only knows a world in which she is in charge. This has made peer relationships challenging for her.

It also seems that, while Kathryn and Kevin report that Sasha acts like she is the best and number one in all things, they sense that it's bravado. Even though Sasha is very smart and skilled, they believe she lacks self-confidence. She needs to brag about how much she knows or how she's the best at everything to cover up for feelings of insecurity. This hypothesis is strengthened when they hear from Sasha's teacher that she is making up stories. Kathryn and Kevin are concerned that Sasha feels the need to exaggerate and embellish to elevate herself.

The Plan

They start setting clearer limits. Kathryn and Kevin realize that one major underlying factor in Sasha's trouble with peers is her inflexibility. It's her way or the highway. They are committed to helping her learn to accept that she can't always have everything the way she wants, and to tune in to other people's thoughts, feelings, and needs. They know this means setting clearer limits and expectations. For example, when Sasha tries to make her mom feel guilty for being on a work call when she wants to play, Kathryn acknowledges that it's hard for Sasha not to have mom whenever she wants, but mom also has other important responsibilities. Kathryn then goes into another room to provide a boundary so she can make her call. She doesn't react to Sasha's protests and her banging on the door. When Kathryn is done, she tells Sasha she did a great job waiting (even if she has been protesting the entire time) and moves on to show it's all good—they both survived a difficult moment. Taking steps like this helps Sasha learn to accept that other people have needs that must be respected.

They stop showering Sasha with constant praise. Kathryn and Kevin realize they have gone overboard telling Sasha how everything she does is the best and most wonderful. They now see that Sasha is internalizing all of this praise as a belief that she is always being evaluated and always has to be tops. Instead, they focus on her efforts versus outcomes and show acceptance for times she is not the winner or the best. When she does the full set of monkey bars and seeks praise, they respond: "You worked so hard to build your strength to get all the way across—how does that feel?" Versus, "You are amazing! We are so proud of you! You are the best at the monkey bars!" When she doesn't make a goal in soccer and starts putting down her teammates and blaming them for the loss, instead of saying, "But you were great out there!" they respond: "It's hard to lose. Everyone struggles with that." This addresses and validates the underlying issue she's truly struggling with. It also shows that they will pay attention to and value her no matter her performance.

They stop shaming her. They avoid making statements like, "Nobody is going to want to play with you when you boss them around," or labeling her as "mean."

They address Sasha wanting one friend all to herself. They avoid going out of the gate telling Sasha what to do as they know that would likely be met with defensiveness. Instead, they start by validating

Sasha's experience—that she likes having Reagan all to herself. Then Kathryn tells her a story:

> *I had a good friend, Mia, whom I loved. We played a lot together. And there were also times when I wanted to do something different than she did, like ride my bike when she wanted to do art. I also wanted to play with other kids in my class and neighborhood. I wasn't rejecting her—I still loved her, and she was always one of my best friends. It turns out that sometimes kids just want to play something different. It's not that they don't like you or want to play with you anymore; it's that they want to do another activity or play with other kids. I wonder if that might be what's happening with your friend. Sounds like you need to decide if you can you get comfortable with playing with Reagan along with some other friends too. That's up to you. What choice do you think would work out better for you?*

They guide Sasha to assess the outcome of her unsuccessful encounters with peers. They engage her in being social detectives to analyze what happened and what might lead to a different outcome:

- "What happened when you try to make Emma do what you want her to do?"

- "What happened when you told your friend that she was stupid for not wanting to play the game you wanted to play? Did that work out the way you wanted? What might you do next time?"

- "It sounds like if you want your friends to play with you, you'll have to think about whether you can be flexible and include their ideas in your play—to take turns playing different roles and letting other people go first, sometimes. What do you think you want to do? What would turn out best for you when it comes to playing with friends?"

These kinds of conversations ("meetings") via FaceTime or Zoom can be very effective, like Chris and Amanda did with Nico in chapter 3. You go into separate spaces and have the discussion remotely. This can reduce the discomfort some kids experience in face-to-face encounters. It's silly and fun. It takes some of the pressure off and opens them up.

The Outcome

As hard as it is to stay consistent with the limits and tolerate Sasha's upset, Kathryn and Kevin are seeing a significant, positive shift with Sasha not only being more flexible but also being less irritable and combative, overall.

On the social front, there is good news. Kathryn reports:

Sasha had a friend over. They were doing well for a while. Then I hear Sasha saying to this other girl that she is "dumb, a maniac, stupid" and a whole lot of other horrible things. The friend found me and told me she wanted to leave. I stayed calm and told Sasha that it was time for us to have a meeting. Sasha had loved this idea of having meetings to discuss important matters. It made her feel very grown-up and reduced her defensiveness. When we were alone, I told Sasha that I could see she was having a hard time being kind to her friend and that she had "two great choices": she could turn the "mean" off, be kind, and see if her friend would like to stay; or, she could keep being unkind and her friend would need to leave. I told Sasha that I knew this was a really big decision—that she might be very disappointed if her friend had to leave—so I would give her a whole two minutes to decide what she wanted to do. She stormed away and slammed the door to her room. I didn't react. She came back out less than a minute later and said she wanted her friend to stay. Sasha couldn't face her directly or apologize. So, I asked the friend if she would let Sasha try again. The friend said okay, and Sasha was amazing for the rest of the afternoon. They had a blast.

I know it doesn't always work out so swimmingly. When it doesn't, it's not a failure and doesn't mean that the approach isn't useful. It's a developmentally appropriate, respectful, supportive, and loving way to handle these thorny situations, even when the outcome is not exactly as you had hoped. It sends the right message and creates an opportunity for your child to figure out what kind of friend they want to be. It's a process and the effects are cumulative. Stay the course.

Jackson Experiences Exclusion

The Presenting Problem

Jackson (seven) comes home from school in tears. He explains to his parents, Alicia and Harlan, that he is being treated badly by a classmate, Owen. Owen teases and excludes him in the aftercare program. Alicia has contacted the school to be sure they're aware of what's going on and that they will intervene. They learn that there aren't any issues in the classroom. The challenges are only during aftercare where there is less structure, and the supervisors are not as skilled as the teachers in managing social challenges.

Alicia and Harlan are very worried about Jackson and contact me for guidance on how they can best support him as parents. They explain that Jackson is a very sweet and sensitive child. He doesn't have a mean bone in his body. He is attracted to Owen because he is very popular and sporty, even though Jackson is not into team sports and prefers reading and being creative. He likes doing art and building things. They have tried to point out to Jackson that he shouldn't care about Owen because he's just a mean kid who doesn't even like the things Jackson likes. He should just stay away from him. But that's not working. Jackson keeps trying to gain Owen's acceptance and to be included. They ask him why he would put himself in a situation to continue being rejected? Why not play with other kids? He says that Owen is getting all of the kids to reject him, so there is no one left to play with. Alicia and Harlan feel stuck about how to help him.

The Analysis

It's a terrible feeling to know your child is being mistreated and that you can't just make it go away, which is exactly what Alicia wants to do. She has thought about taking Jackson out of aftercare, but this would be a logistical nightmare and costly for their family. More importantly, Alicia knows that this will not be the only time Jackson encounters situations like this and that he needs to learn how to deal with them. She can't fight his battles. She needs to arm him with the confidence and tools to work through them in a positive way.

The Plan

- **They lead with empathy.** Alicia and Harlan validate the difficulty of this social dynamic, especially since Owen is getting other kids to join his "team" against Jackson. It's a lot to think about and, as his helpers, they will support him in figuring out the best way to handle it.

- **They engage Jackson in being investigators.** The idea is to interest him in learning about why kids exclude others. They suspect he will like this a lot because he is very cerebral and scientifically minded. Alicia and Harlan do some research in advance to find resources that are appropriate for helping seven-year-olds understand why kids might act in hurtful ways, which they share with Jackson. Together, they learn that kids often tease and exclude because they have their own insecurities and a need for power and control. They target kids who have big reactions because that's what they're looking for. Alicia and Harlan use this information to emphasize to Jackson that it's not a reflection on him and ask what he thinks would be best for him moving forward. Without an agenda or trying to sway him, they say that it looks like he has some options. He can continue to try to gain Owen's acceptance, but he may keep getting rejected because that's what gives Owen power. Or Jackson can ignore Owen and find other things to do in aftercare. They offer to brainstorm other options.

- **They collaborate with the aftercare program supervisors.** The staff agrees to provide more structure that includes splitting up Owen's group and assigning kids partners for projects. This will provide opportunities for Jackson to engage one-on-one with his peers without Owen's interference. They also share that there are lots of other kids in the program whom Jackson can engage with—Owen hasn't wrangled all the kids into his circle. They identify other kids who might be a good fit for Jackson—who aren't super into sports and are more artistic and intellectual. Alicia plans playdates with some of these kids to give Jackson a chance to build relationships that can extend to school.

The Outcome

Jackson is eager to have playdates with some of the kids from aftercare on the weekends. This helps a lot, especially because he is less focused on seeking acceptance from Owen. Slowly, some of the other kids who had joined Owen's group show interest in connecting with Jackson again. Alicia and Harlan also plan playdates with these kids to help solidify these relationships. Taking these steps has resulted in Jackson not only feeling better about his social relationships but also experiencing less stress and more joy overall.

OTHER COMMON SCENARIOS

When Kids Make Fun of Other Kids

Children who have a low tolerance for "failing" or feeling vulnerable tend to tease others when *they* fail. They might laugh at a peer who misses a ball that's thrown to them or gives the wrong answer to a question at school. Their own feelings of self-doubt and insecurity are triggered when they see peers struggling. Projecting these feelings onto others is a way to cope with emotions that are difficult to tolerate.

When you see your child teasing others, your knee-jerk reaction may be to come down on them for being unkind. But that can backfire. The shame children experience when being reprimanded shuts them down. They become defensive, which leads neither to learning nor to positive change.

An effective way to respond when your child makes fun of others is to introduce the idea of being social detectives together. This helps them think through these encounters without criticism or judgment:

- "Malcolm missed the goal. How do you think that made him feel?"
- "What's it like for you when you make a mistake or don't do something perfectly?"
- "How do you think Malcolm felt when you made fun of him for missing the goal?"

Taking this approach opens children up to reflect on their actions, which makes them more likely to change their mindset and thus their behavior.

You might share your own stories: "I was not so great at math and felt embarrassed about it. I had a friend who was really good at math, and I felt really jealous of her. I wanted to tease her when she made a mistake because I thought it would make me feel better. But it didn't; it felt bad inside. And she stopped wanting to play with me. So, I decided to stop teasing and just work harder on my math!"

You can also build your child's empathy by sensitively recalling a time when they struggled: "Remember when you were working so hard to ride a two-wheeler and got really mad every time you fell? You didn't like the feeling of not being perfect at it right away. That's hard for a lot of people, including me! How would you feel if someone had teased you for wobbling or falling? Would that give you good or bad feelings about that person?"

You conclude with leaving it in your child's hands: "What's so great is that you are your own person, and you get to decide how you are with your friends—whether you want them to have good feelings about you and to feel good about yourself as a friend, or not. That's up to you."

When Your Child Acts as if They Lack Empathy

Parents frequently report that their children laugh, refuse to make eye contact, cover their ears, run away, or get hostile and angry when they are confronted about their unkind behavior. These moms and dads are mortified and worried, wondering how they could be raising a child who doesn't appear to feel bad about doing harm or, worse, who gains pleasure from it. Herein lies one of the most challenging aspects of childrearing: as adults, we tend to interpret children's behavior through the lens of logic. Some parents worry that when their child laughs or acts as if they don't care that they have done or said something hurtful, it means they have no empathy and may be a budding sociopath.

But we can't ascribe adult logic to children's behavior. While their actions may seem irrational and concerning at face value, the meaning of these behaviors becomes clear and makes sense when you look at it from the child's perspective. Laughing, turning or running away, and covering their ears are all coping mechanisms that provide protection and relief from a flood of difficult emotions—to stop you from saying things that make them uncomfortable. Facing your anger or disappointment about their behavior can be overwhelming for HSCs. Cognitively, they know they have done something unacceptable, but they don't have the skills yet to stop themselves from acting on their impulses. They engage in all sorts of evasions to distract from the stress and discomfort of these encounters. They are trying to cope with feelings that are difficult to process and manage.

This is also why many HSCs are allergic to saying "sorry." Apologizing means acknowledging that they have acted hurtfully, which floods them with shame and they shut down or get dysregulated and even act silly—all signs of discomfort, not sociopathy. In fact, many of these unwanted behaviors result not from a lack of empathy but, rather, from an abundance of it. Because of how tuned in they are to others' feelings and how deeply they care, their shame is exponential.

What You Can Do

- **Lead with empathy.** "You're a great kid who had a tough moment." This lets your child know you aren't angry or criticizing them, which makes it more likely they will connect and absorb the messages you want to share.
- **Don't try to force or demand your child make eye contact.** You may find it rude and disrespectful when your child won't look you in the eye when you are trying to communicate with them. But I don't recommend trying to force your child to make eye contact because it can backfire. In these moments, children are trying to protect themselves from uncomfortable feelings of shame about their behavior and

your palpable disappointment in them. Looking you in the eye can feel overwhelming. Demanding they do so only increases their stress and makes it more likely they will get further dysregulated—laugh, become silly, run, or turn away—or just shut down.

Further, making a demand that you have no control over (you can't actually make your child look you in the eye) just promulgates a power struggle that takes on a life of its own and the whole point of your direction or correction is subjugated.

- **Instead, acknowledge your child's discomfort.** "It's hard to think and talk about tough stuff. I know."
- **Matter-of-factly state what happened.** "You were frustrated and pushed Marnie. Your body acted before your brain. You feel bad; you didn't mean to be hurtful."
- **Offer to help them think it through.** "When you're ready, I'm happy to help you think about what happened and if you want to do something to make it better."

Setting Limits Without Shame

While you can't force your child to be kind, you can set limits that prevent them from acting in ways that are not healthy for them or others. Here is a model I developed to implement limits in these situations that avoids shame and punishment. It can be used in any group situation, inside and outside the home.

Start by explaining that anytime we are with other people, we are in a group, even if it's just one other person. When we are alone, we are solo. There are different rules for being with groups and being solo. For example, in a group, there is a need to take turns, to be respectful while other people are talking, and to use kind words and gentle bodies. If anyone is having a hard time following the group rules, it means they need solo time in a space where they are free to use their voices and bodies however they like. Offer examples, like a child having to take a break from the sandbox at the park if they're throwing sand or are not willing to share the shovels.

Caleb's parents use this approach to address the teasing. They acknowledge that it's Caleb's voice and he is the only one who decides how to use it—to say kind or unkind things. When he chooses kindness, he gets to keep playing in the group. When he uses his voice in hurtful ways, he needs some solo time.

Sasha's parents use it too. When they hear her being unkind, they take her aside—so they are not embarrassing her in front of her friend—and tell her that they have some important information to share. To avoid a defensive reaction, they don't correct her and, instead, say: "You have two great choices: you can switch gears and be kind; or you can take three minutes of solo time to have a chance to regroup and try again." If Sasha needs solo time, they explain to her friend that everyone is getting a few minutes of break time before they return to play, and they give that child something they can do on their own.

WHEN TO SEEK HELP

If social challenges are interfering on a regular basis in your child's ability to form positive friendships, it's important to seek the support of a child development expert who can help you assess what kind of intervention would be most helpful. Lots of kids participate in social skills groups that many psychotherapy practices offer that can be very productive.

RELATIONSHIPS WITH SIBLINGS

Haha—you lost!

Stop singing that stupid song. You're hurting my ears!

You cannot play this game! You don't know how to play!

If you intentionally had multiple children, you likely did so because you want your kids to have a sibling(s) to grow up with and to be fierce and be a loyal lifelong companion. You dreamed your children would be best friends. Then reality hits: the older child struggles with intense jealousy when the baby is born and has frequent meltdowns when you can't focus all your attention on them. As your kids grow, there is constant squabbling. One child is mean and says horrible things to their brother or sister. The fighting can get physical and become very disruptive to the whole family system. If you have wondered what you were thinking having that second, third, or fourth child, you are not alone.

The sibling relationship is about as complex as it gets. It triggers a confluence of emotions that runs the gamut from the extremes of love to hate and back again. The natural conflict that arises as siblings navigate their relationship ranks as one of the most vexing challenges for parents in my practice. Yet this conflict happens for good reason.

The sibling relationship is the testing ground for building all sorts of skills for getting along with others: how to share, take turns, cope with jealousy and competition, build empathy, and learn to collaborate and jointly resolve problems. So, try not to fear the conflicts between your children. When you position yourself as a facilitator of this process, versus a solver of all problems, it can reduce conflict and make it more likely that your children will ultimately learn to respect, value, and even adore each other.

It starts with making some key mindshifts that address common challenging dynamics that arise, especially when one (or more) of your children is a big reactor.

MINDSHIFTS

Manage your expectations. Conflict will happen, a lot. It doesn't mean your children will never get along or become fast friends.

Expect irrationality. The feelings triggered between siblings are often intense and irrational, rooted in deep-seated emotions of competition and jealousy that kids don't have conscious access to. Here's a personal tale I am not proud of, but which serves as a good example. After more than five hundred consecutive nights of Sam deciding what books we read at bedtime, Jess finally had the language to announce that she wanted a chance to choose and blurted out: "*Good Dog Carl!*" I naturally responded: "Great choice, Jess! Of course you get a chance to pick a book." (I mean, the score was five hundred to zero.) Sam's response: "I never get to choose the books!" I looked at him in total disbelief and responded: "What in the world are you talking about? You have chosen bedtime books every night for two years!" The more I tried to reason with him, the more outrageous and vehement his protests. I was at a loss as to how to get him to see life through the lens of logic!

My calmer, wiser, twenty-twenty-hindsight self knows that this was a very insensitive and unhelpful reaction. Sam was triggered by the unexpected change in the routine and did not yet have the ability to cope with it. Responding with anger and rejection was decidedly not a positive parenting strategy.

How would I respond if I had a do-over? "Wow! Jess can use her words now to let us know what she's thinking. And she wants a chance to choose books. That's a big change because you got to pick all the books for so long—almost two years! I know you don't like it, and that's okay. I don't expect you to. It's my job to make sure both of you have a chance to choose books, so we will be alternating from now on: you choose books one night, Jess chooses the next." If Sam had continued to protest, I would have kept moving on to show that I could tolerate his upset but would be sticking with the limit.

In these moments, what kids need is acknowledgment of their feelings—which are not right or wrong, good or bad—*and* appropriate limits. Trying to convince my four-year-old about the fairness of this new plan only intensified his stance. I was not meeting him where he was understandably at. Being the sole selector of bedtime books had been his lived experience so far and all he had ever known. Learning to share and take turns with a sibling was a difficult adjustment. But that's one of the benefits of having a sibling: accepting that others have needs and that you can survive not getting everything you want exactly when and how you want it. That is a true gift that keeps on giving.

Your job is not to make your kids get along; that's something you have no control over. *Your job is to help them learn to get along.* It's your job to ensure your kids are physically and emotionally safe—you will not let anyone in the family be harmful with their words or actions. It's your children's job to figure out how they want to play and be with each other. Trying to control the sibling relationship often results in more, not less, rivalry. Instead, see yourself as a facilitator whose job it is to help your children learn to manage their own conflict and engage in a mutually satisfying way.

CASES

Disgruntled Diego

The Presenting Problem

Marco and Hannah are frustrated and concerned about the level of sibling conflict between their kids—Diego (six), a big reactor, and Zara (three). They can happily play for long periods and Diego can be a great big brother. But he also does a lot of taunting and teasing. He can be aggressive when he's angry at Zara for not playing the way he wants or when he feels she is intruding into his space or with his things. The level of conflict is having a very negative effect on their family life.

The Analysis

This one doesn't take much analysis. Sibling rivalry exists in most families to some degree and is often more intense and pervasive when there's a big reactor in the mix. This isn't surprising given that HSCs register and react to their experiences in the world more intensely. They tend to be more jealous and competitive with their siblings, which is the case with Diego, who is a highly spirited little guy who runs very hot and can go from zero to sixty in a split second. This makes it really difficult for Marco and Hannah to anticipate when he might explode.

The Plan

Hannah and Marco normalize sibling conflict. During dinner one night, Hannah and Marco tell stories about their own siblings—fun times they had as kids as well as conflicts. Diego and Zara are fascinated to hear about their parents' experiences and ask lots of questions.

They explain that experiencing a range of feelings about one's siblings is totally normal; sometimes they are going to adore each other and have the best time together. Other times they are going to be jealous, competitive, and annoyed at having to share, take turns, and so on. Giving voice to this phenomenon can be validating for kids who may be confused and overwhelmed by the big, mixed feelings about their siblings that are hard to make sense of and manage. This means that Hannah and Marco no longer make statements like, "But you love your sister!" when Diego is expressing angry feelings about Zara, which usually backfires and results in him more vehemently asserting his animosity toward her. Now they respond: "You love Zara sometimes and other times are annoyed with her because she messes with your stuff. Having those mixed feelings makes a lot of sense. It's also hard to learn to share mommy and daddy with your sister. It gives you negative feelings about her when she's getting our attention because you want all of it, like it used to be before she was born. We totally get that and will help you learn to share us with her. That's our job."

They teach the kids about expectations for being part of a group. Hannah and Marco explain that their family is a group because it includes several people. Just like at school, where they are also part of a group, the most important rule is that everyone uses safe bodies and safe words. When kids are having trouble doing that, then they take solo time, also known as a solo/safe space break, where they are free to use their voices and bodies however they like. This keeps everyone safe. They engage the kids by asking for examples of what happens in school when a child throws toys, hits or kicks other kids, screams loudly for a long time, or says mean things to their classmates. They all agree that the teacher helps the child take a break to calm their bodies so they can rejoin the class. That's what Hannah and Marco will be doing for them. (See the appendix for resources on how to set up and implement safe space breaks.)

They are clear that this isn't punishment, it's a teaching tool and a necessary boundary to ensure safety for all. The solo/safe space will include soothing activities—such as Play-Doh, threading beads, a kiddie tent, a beanbag chair, and safe items to squish and throw—to help them get back to a zone where they can engage in a positive way. They incorporate the concept of the "two great choices": "I hear someone saying 'stop!' What's our family rule about that? We respect others people's bodies and space. You have two great choices: you can stop on your own or we will help you stop." This sometimes means giving Diego a break if they can't get him to stop the unwanted behavior.

Making the determination about when you use the solo/safe space can be tricky. Hannah and Marco decide, for example, that, when Diego pushes Zara, it doesn't necessarily mean he needs solo time. Instead, they respond: "Do you need to push? We'll help you find something to push safely. We don't push people because people have feelings. I know you are mad that Zara took one of your puzzle pieces. She is still learning how to control her body. But pushing can be dangerous and is not okay." If Diego is able to move forward safely, they carry on. If Diego spirals and continues to be aggressive, then they help him to the solo/safe space break: "It looks like you're having a hard time working this out. Time for a break. You can try again in five minutes." The solo/safe space includes a boundary. This is essential to prevent Diego from running out and getting himself more revved up, which would escalate the situation.

The reason I developed this solo/safe space strategy is that parents need a positive way to stay in charge and be the rock their kids need them to be. This can't happen when parents are unable to ensure safety and when they aren't able to get their kids back in control. The solo/safe space empowers parents to end an unhealthy situation and not leave the outcome in their children's hands.

They teach Diego and Zara to solve their problems themselves. Hannah and Marco explain that when Diego and Zara are having a hard time, they will help by using a handy tool called "pause and problem-solve." When they hear unkind words or see either of them using their body in harmful ways, they will clearly announce, "Pause, people" to cue them to freeze. Then they will name the problem: "I see you are having a hard time sharing the trucks." Or "You have different ideas for how to build the castle." They will ask for their ideas and suggest other options, if necessary. Hannah and Marco are clear that they are not going to solve the problem for them. They are just helping them think through the situation to see if, together as siblings, they can come up with a solution so they can keep playing.

One great strategy for kids three and older is to give them five minutes to conduct their own "meeting" to figure out a plan to solve the problem. Then, they present their solution to you. If it's acceptable, they can go on their merry way and continue playing. The beauty of this strategy is that, in order to keep playing together or have access to a desired toy, they need to collaborate.

Your job is to facilitate—to guide your children to solve their own problems: "Two kids, one pterodactyl. Hmm . . . how can we solve this problem?" If they can't come to some agreement, the toy can take a "toy time-out." Explain that you will let them try again after whatever period of time you think makes sense. Once kids see that you are not going to solve their problems, and that lack of collaboration on their part is going to lead to a loss for both of them, they are often more motivated to share and take turns.

They provide opportunities when the kids don't have to share. Hannah and Marco make a rule that if one child wants to work on something on their own, they have to go into the separate, "solo" space (which might be their bedroom) because the family or "group" spaces are for sharing. If Diego wants to build a block structure and doesn't want Zara to knock it down, he can erect it in his room or some other space where there can be a boundary.

They also allow the kids to choose (within reason) some toys that they don't have to share. The caveat is that when they want to play with these toys, and they don't want to share them, they do so in their "solo" space.

They don't fall into the black hole of trying to untangle what transpired—the "he said, she said" vortex. Instead, Marco and Hannah listen to each child's perspective and then restate them without judgment: "It's hard when your sister has a different idea about how to build the tower." "You thought Diego was done with the superhero cape and you wanted a turn." This helps each child put themselves in the other's shoes.

They avoid acting as referees. When there is a conflict, Hannah and Marco stay neutral. They name the problem and move to facilitate finding solutions. "Sounds like you guys are having a hard time deciding what roles to play. Zara, you don't like that Diego is saying that you always have to be the baby dinosaur, and he is the big one. You can decide to take turns playing different roles or decide not to play. What do you think you want to do?" Remember, your children need to figure out how they are going to work out these conflicts. If you become the decider, you are interfering in that process. Taking sides or protecting one child from another plays right into and escalates the rivalry. It also creates a dynamic where one child is the "aggressor" and the other the "victim"—roles kids internalize and which can, over time, get solidified and define the sibling relationship in the long term.

They don't shame the "perpetrator." Hannah and Marco stop making statements that demonize the child who is being the aggressor, such as: "Why would you want to hurt your sister?" "What's wrong with you?" These kinds of responses usually make things worse as they reinforce the reputation of the shamed child, in this case, Diego, as the "difficult" one. The maligned child feels resentful and, thus, is more likely to act out toward their siblings and others. Further, shaming results in kids shutting down and becoming evasive, which interferes in their ability to learn better ways of dealing with conflict—the ultimate goal. It does nothing to support their ability to make better choices as they grow.

They focus more on the behavior they want to see than on the infraction. Hannah and Marco have found that focusing on the wrongdoing tends to backfire and only increases negative behavior. When Diego gets rough with Zara, they say: "It looks like you need a way to get your energy out. Here are some soft balls to smash, throw or bang." Providing an option for solving the problem versus spending a lot of time on the violation tends to put children in a more positive state of mind and makes it more likely they will make a positive course correction.

They create a "cueing" system to try to preempt the aggressive behavior. They act as helpers by having each child come up with a word that Marco or Hannah will say when Diego or Zara are heading down an unacceptable path. Zara's word is "Peppa." When she's provoking Diego, not listening to his pleas to get out of the way when he is throwing a ball into a basket, Hannah says: "Is there a Peppa here who needs a big hug?" Diego's word is "Pluto." When he is teasing Zara, saying she's a "stupid baby" when she won't play the game he wants to play, Marco says: "Is that Pluto, I said Pluuuuto, orbiting Earth right now?" It's a loving and supportive way to try to throw a monkey wrench into the behavior that's brewing.

They role-play to give the kids practice resolving challenges. Hannah and Marco explain they are doing an experiment to learn how to resolve problems. They engage the kids in making a list of typical conflicts. Hannah and Marco choose the one they'll start with (knowing if they leave it up to the kids to decide, it will just start a new conflict). Then they have the kids act it out, which they mostly find very funny, easing the tension. Hannah and Marco use the "pause and problem-solve" approach during these role-plays to give them practice with this tool. When Hannah and Marco say "pause," everyone freezes, and they go into problem-solving mode to see if they can resolve the issue.

After they play out each conflict, the kids do an assessment and the parents take notes: Were they able to solve the problem? If so, how? If not, what was the obstacle? What could they do differently next time? They give the kids a chance to redo the conflicts they couldn't resolve. The idea is to give Diego and Zara an opportunity to practice conflict-resolution strategies outside the actual heat of the moment.

To incentivize, Hannah and Marco explain that when a conflict arises in real life and the kids can resolve the problem, they can add five minutes to silly sibling time—jumping on mom and dad's bed—before bathtime. If they can't resolve it, everyone takes a five-minute break in separate spaces to chill out and regroup.

The Outcome

Diego and Zara love the role-playing. Practicing the "pause-and-problem-solve" approach and using the cue words is making a big, positive impact. When they have a conflict, Hannah and Marco will interject: "Hmm, what did we learn from our detective work about resolving conflicts?" This often sets the kids on a better course.

Even when none of the problem-solving strategies work, Hannah and Marco find that things aren't escalating as quickly or intensely.

They see that avoiding playing the referee is helping. They are often able to give the kids a mutual break—with both going to a separate space, not necessarily the solo space, to take a breather.

When a child, usually Diego, needs a solo/safe space break, it's not easy. Marco often must physically move him there because Diego is so out of control. Marco stays on the other side of the door, and when Diego counts to ten, that signals he's ready to rejoin the group. The big difference is now Marco and Zara don't hold on to anger and are dealing with these situations more dispassionately. They emphasize to Diego how much they want him to be with the group. They are effusive about what a great job he does calming himself in a difficult moment. They note that everybody is still learning how to deal with their big feelings so they can be the best family member they can be.

Junie the Constant Controller

The Presenting Problem

Andrew and Alesia are very concerned about their family dynamic. They have a very intense big reactor, Junie (seven), and two younger kids: Robby (five), who is easier going, and Hudson (thirteen months). Junie's demands, meltdowns, and inflexibility control everyone. Andrew and Alesia feel like they can't go anywhere because Junie gets easily triggered when things don't go her way. She is constantly making accusations that she is not getting enough attention. Everything is unfair. She insists on always being first and on making all the decisions for the family: which playground to go to, which restaurant to eat at, which show to watch, and so on. Everything must be the way she wants it. Andrew and Alesia feel that no matter the lengths they go to give Junie the attention she wants, or to adapt to her demands, it will never be enough. She is "sucking the oxygen out of our entire family," laments Alesia, who is particularly exhausted because Junie has a strong preference for mom and demands her constant attention. "She is my bottomless pit." Alesia tears up as she shares her sadness over not feeling she has given the baby what she needs and hasn't had nearly the time she wants with Robby because she is so busy reacting to Junie. She is also angry at Junie for putting her in this situation.

Andrew and Alesia are also troubled that Robby is now compromising his own needs to pacify Junie. They have been rationalizing (hoping) that he doesn't mind because he is just so good natured, and the bottom line is that it makes life easier. But deep down, they know this isn't a fair or healthy dynamic. They worry about Robby becoming the "pleaser" and that he may end up feeling resentful of his more reactive, demanding sibling.

The Analysis

This dynamic is very common in families with a child who is a big reactor. Parents are stressed and exhausted and often take, as one dad called it, "the parenting path of least resistance"—adapting to the demands of their big reactor to head off arguments and explosions. The energy and self-control it takes for parents to set the limits and tolerate their HSCs' persistence, constant badgering, and meltdowns feels impossible. But absent limits, big reactors don't learn to be more flexible, and the detrimental dynamic persists.

This situation is not only harmful to Andrew, Alesia, Robby, and Hudson but is, in fact, also not good for Junie to be the lightning rod in the family—to have the power to derail the family and be the target of constant anger and annoyance. Andrew and Alesia see that walking on eggshells around Junie is unhealthy. They realize that they can't make parenting decisions based on fear and avoidance of her meltdowns when things don't go her way.

They also see that they need to address Junie's preference and efforts to monopolize all of Alesia. While HSCs are known to make fierce attachments and thus, develop these strong preferences, it's giving Alesia very negative feelings about Junie. It's also amplifying the sibling rivalry as Junie's brother and sister are seen as constant competitors for Alesia's affection and attention. This is not helping Junie learn to tolerate not getting all the attention and accept that other's needs are important too—a critical aspect of long-term, healthy psychological development.

The Plan

They start to set appropriate limits with Junie. Think back to Nico, featured in chapter 3, where a similar family dynamic is at play with Nico sucking out all of the oxygen from the family. Andrew and Alesia take a similar approach to the one Amanda and Chris implement. Accordingly, they acknowledge Junie's desire to always be first but don't enable it. They make a new nighttime schedule that has Andrew and Alesia rotating the child they are putting to bed. They institute having the kids take turns choosing restaurants and playgrounds.

They don't let Robby sacrifice himself to keep the peace.

- "Robby, I know you want to be a helper by doing Junie's job, but you both have a responsibility to put your own dishes in the sink. It's a mommy/daddy job to make sure you each learn to do that."

- "Robby, I know it's hard to see Junie so upset about not going to her favorite playground, but it's your turn to choose so we are going to stick with that. It's our job to help Junie cope with this disappointment, which can be really hard."

- "You are a great brother but making it all better for Junie isn't your responsibility or good for her. She is smart and strong and will be okay. She's got what it takes."

They help Robby understand his highly sensitive sibling. They start by acknowledging Robby's lived experience while not disparaging Junie. They want to build empathy and understanding. They include the following messages:

- Our brains control our actions. When we're hungry, our brain tells our hand to reach for an apple. When we feel love for someone, our brain tells our arms to give them a big hug.

- We all have different brains. They don't all work the same. They talk about lots of different people they know and how they all react to the same experiences differently. Alesia shares: "Daddy loves big, group activities with lots of action. I get overwhelmed in those kinds of situations and prefer just being with one or two people in quieter places. You like to jump right into new things. Your friend, Roopa, needs more time to feel comfortable with an experience that's not familiar to her. That's why she cried a lot the first few days of school. We all have different brains and bodies; that's why we react differently to the same experiences." They go on to explain that some brains are really good at staying calm, even when something difficult or upsetting happens, like his brain. "Other brains, like Junie's, have a harder time staying calm. Her body and words sometimes act before her brain. She doesn't mean to be hurtful. We are helping Junie manage her really big feelings."

The Outcome

It's really hard for Andrew and Alesia to tolerate Junie's upset at not being able to control everything, but they are getting better at it and are motivated to stay the course because they are seeing positive changes:

- Junie is still protesting a lot, but she calms and adapts more quickly when she sees her parents are holding firm.
- When she gets disruptive—screaming at the top of her lungs in the middle of the family room or being destructive when her body acts before her brain—they guide her to her solo/break space. Experiencing this natural consequence more often than not results in her being able to stop and course correct.
- When she insists on having mom at bedtime when it's dad's turn, Andrew doesn't react to her rejection. He lets her know he is happy to read and cuddle with her when she's ready and then gives her space. He keeps the door locked while they are in her bedroom so she can't go running out to find Alesia and create more havoc. With these clear limits, bedtimes are becoming easier. (See the appendix for resources on solving sleep challenges.)

Having a plan for what to do when Junie has a hard time outside the home is more challenging because they have less control. But they're figuring it out, as illustrated by this encounter they share. They met Alesia's sister, Giselle, and her family at one of their favorite restaurants. Giselle gave Junie and her same-age cousin, Haley, Troll bags. Haley's bag featured characters from the most recent Troll movie, Junie's didn't. Junie had a major meltdown. She started shouting and tried to grab Haley's bag. Previously, Alesia and Andrew would have spent a long time trying to get Junie to accept her bag. They might even have tried to broker a deal for Haley to give Junie the desired bag, hoping to end this miserable moment. If Junie couldn't get back in control, they likely would have collected all the kids and left.

But on this day, once they saw that Junie was in red zone and not reachable, Andrew calmly told her that he would be a helper and carried her to the car, locked the doors so she couldn't run out, put on her favorite music, and then remained a quiet presence. He explained he would sit with her until she was calm; then they could go back to join the family because that is the rule at restaurants—everyone has to use inside voices and calm bodies. Within five minutes, Junie calmed. They returned to the family. Junie not only had a pleasurable remainder of the dinner but was also in a very upbeat mood when they got home. Our hypothesis/hope is that being able to get back into control and muscle through that difficult moment gave Junie very positive feelings about herself. It was all made possible by Alesia and Andrew staying calm and providing the containment/boundaries Junie needed to regroup, without any shaming, punishing, or adding fuel to her flame.

FINAL THOUGHTS

If the sibling conflict is a constant interference in your family's everyday functioning—to the point that you rarely feel you can all spend time together peacefully and joyfully—and that you always have to divide and conquer, consider contacting a child development or family therapist to help surface the underlying issues and address the dynamics with the support of a professional.

8

Understanding and Addressing Other Common Issues

WHEN YOUR CHILD ENGAGES IN NEGATIVE SELF-TALK

I am so stupid.

Nobody likes me.

You don't love me. You don't want me in this family.

Understandably, parents find these kinds of statements disturbing. But it's important to keep in mind that in these moments, children don't necessarily mean *exactly* what they say. They are in a highly charged state, flooded with big emotions that are difficult to experience and process. What they are actually struggling with—the meaning behind the words—may not be readily apparent to you *or* them. We can't be in our children's brains and know exactly why they are saying something so alarming. What are they experiencing and trying to communicate?

But it's important that you seek to understand the underlying issues and, most importantly, what your child needs from you to work through the distress conveyed in these statements.

It requires us to manage our own anxiety in these moments. Big reactions can overwhelm children and shut them down. Remind yourself that it's a sign that your child trusts you and feels safe to share their deepest feelings with you. This can help you stay calm and be present for your child in the way they need you to be, and to tune in to what they are communicating through these distressing statements. That will give you the best chance to help your child work through these difficult feelings and experiences—the ultimate goal.

Why Children Engage in Negative Self-Talk

Your child's words may have a range of meanings. Context matters a lot. Here are some common underlying factors at play when kids are making self-deprecating or worrying statements.

They are experiencing big feelings that they can't process or manage effectively. Your child might be overwhelmed with sadness, fear, or anger that they are purging. Samantha (six) is very slow to warm up and has just started first grade at a new school. Mornings are challenging for her. Samantha is expressing anxiety through her inability to choose what to wear. When her parents put pressure on her to decide, she blurts out, "I wish I wasn't alive." We suspect that what she means is that she wishes her really big feelings would disappear.

Millie (four) blurts out "Why do you hate me?" when her mom explains that she can't read a book to her at that moment because she has to feed the baby. Her parents are pretty sure these proclamations aren't accurate reflections of her true feelings; rather, she is expressing her jealousy of the attention her new brother is getting. These are very hard feelings for a young child to manage, so they get expressed in extreme ways.

Their feelings are all-encompassing and globalized. In response to her dad asking about her day at school, Allie (seven) says: "Nobody likes me. I have no friends." It turns out that Allie was not chosen that day to be a team captain in soccer. She often looks at the world from a black/white, all-or-nothing perspective. She can be having a great day; then she has one stressful or difficult experience and all is wrong with the world.

They don't like a limit you are setting. It's time for lights-out. Logan (six) is mad that his dad, Peter, won't tell him one more story. Logan accuses Peter of not loving him, saying things like, "Mom loves me more. You don't even want me to be in this family!" This results in Peter staying longer and longer to appease Logan and prove his love. Bedtime is extending way too long. Peter feels manipulated and resentful. The loving bedtime routine turns into a tense, unloving encounter.

I've heard countless stories and seen hours of video of kids accusing their moms and dads of not loving them when they are unhappy about a limit their parents set. They claim their mom or dad is being mean or somehow wronging them. Ben (five) shouts: "How does it feel to be a bad mom?" when she sticks to the two choices she has offered for breakfast and won't make him pancakes. She is totally perplexed because she feels like all she does is bend over backward to make Ben happy. She is constantly telling him how much she loves him. In fact, she feels guilty about how much more time she and his dad spend with him—meeting his demands for attention—than they do with Ben's easygoing younger brother.

The fact is that children don't love limits. Their distress at not getting what they want puts them into "downstairs," reactive-brain mode. Their proclamations in those moments are often irrational. They will also employ any strategies that work to derail parents from making corrections or implementing limits because they are strategic (not manipulative). One sure way to accomplish this is to call into question their parents' love or to make a self-deprecating statement like: "You just hate me" or "I can't do anything right!" Kids today are keyed into how important it is to parents that their children know how much they love them. They know if they voice feelings of being unloved, their parents will do an about-face and back off to disprove their child's accusations.

They want attention. Children also quickly figure out that making worrisome, alarming statements trigger a reaction and garner a lot of attention from their parents. Many families have reported that when their children are supposed to be doing a task, making a transition, or are trying to divert attention from a sibling, they will make statements like "Nobody likes me," "I'm not good at anything," or "You love Aiden [their sibling] more than me."

Whatever the underlying meaning of your child's negative statements, it's important that they are heard and that their emotions are validated, not judged. Accepting their feelings and seeking to understand them increases the likelihood that you will uncover and address the true issue at play and help them cope with it productively.

What You Can Do

Validate and seek to understand all feelings. The default for most parents is to talk or cheerlead their child out of these feelings because it's so uncomfortable and painful to think about their child having negative feelings about themselves. Common refrains include:

- "What are you talking about, silly? You are the smartest guy I know."
- "That's not true, everybody likes you."
- "That's crazy! We adore you and love you being part of the family."
- "Don't say you wish you weren't alive. That's terrible. You don't mean that."

But as noted frequently in these pages, minimizing or trying to talk kids out of feelings doesn't help them work through and learn to cope with them in healthy ways. So, if your child says they wish they weren't alive, instead of saying what you might be feeling—"Don't say that! You don't mean that!"—you might respond with, "That's a really big feeling. I am so glad you are sharing it with me. Tell me more. I want to understand." Accepting and mirroring your child's feelings soothes their agitated nervous system and helps them get back to a calmer state. This opens up the possibility that they will be able to take a more objective look at their feelings and experiences.

When parents stop trying to minimize or talk their child out of their feelings and, instead, accept and validate them, their child is satisfied and moves on. They have been heard. That was what they needed. This is not to say that your work is done. The underlying issues that are identified—whether they are coping with jealousy toward a sibling, challenges with peers, or a lack of confidence and self-esteem—still need to be addressed. It just means that you can move beyond the alarming language and get to the heart of the issue.

Don't get defensive and launch into proving how much you love your child. That just validates and gives oxygen to their accusations and is often a red herring. They know you love them. Reacting defensively validates that the issue is about love when it's actually about setting an important limit. We know that setting limits is loving. Kids don't see limits that way. Trying to convince them otherwise is just more fodder for their false narrative.

Speak to the underlying feelings you think your child is trying to express. When your child says something negative about their skills or performance, you might respond: "You don't like the way the letter you wrote looks. You have a different idea about how it should appear. It feels really uncomfortable and distressing to you when you can't do something exactly the way you expect or want it to be. I understand." When they accuse you of not loving them when you're setting a limit, you might respond: "I know you don't like having to stop playing to get ready for bed. I understand." Then follow through with the limit.

Help your child reflect on their feelings and experiences to gain new perspective. When you acknowledge and avoid judging or talking your child out of their feelings, they are more likely to be open to hearing your ideas and perspective:

- *I'm so glad you told me that you think we don't want you in this family. I always want to hear about and understand your feelings. It gives me a chance to share how I really feel. I adore and love you deeply. I see that when I set a limit you don't like, you may be angry with me—that's okay. I don't expect you to like it when I say 'no' to something you want. I love you and need to set limits to be a good mom. That's my job.*

- *It's really hard for you when you can't do something perfectly right away. You put a lot of pressure on yourself and judge yourself harshly. Remember, I have been working on my handwriting for more than thirty years! That's so many more years of practice than you have had since you just started to learn to write last year. I had to work really hard to get good at making letters. Learning anything new means making a lot of mistakes. It takes a lot of practice.*
- *Sometimes feelings can be very painful. You want to make them go away. That turns into a wish that you would go away. If you disappear, maybe the feelings will disappear. I understand. Sitting with difficult feelings is hard but I can help you do that. I am here for you.*

Helping your child develop self-awareness—to gain insight into what makes them tick—is what makes it possible for them to ultimately rethink their perspective and self-assessment.

What Your Child Needs

Think back to Logan, who accuses his dad, Peter, of not loving him when he sets a limit on storytelling time. With the insight that Logan doesn't mean exactly what he says—that bedtime is a difficult transition because he loves his dad and doesn't want their time together to end—Peter is able to be the rock Logan needs in these moments. He no longer engages in irrational debates over his love for Logan. He shows empathy for Logan's experience and feelings and then holds the important limit that he can't expect Logan to like but is what he needs. It goes something like this:

Logan: You love Zelda [his sister] more than me! You just want to be in her room reading.

Peter: I know it's hard to end our special time together. I love it too. It's also my job to make sure you get to bed on time. [Then he leaves.]

Logan shouts all sorts of venom through his door. Peter doesn't react. Within ten minutes, Logan comes downstairs, asks his dad if he'll come tuck him in, which Peter happily does.

Logan [as Peter tucks him in]: "I say that stuff when I'm mad. Sorry."

Seeing the positive outcome of taking this approach, Peter is now applying it to many other similar situations. He is finding that Logan calms much more quickly, is showing much greater self-awareness, and is now starting to take responsibility for his actions.

When to Seek Professional Help

If your child persists in making threats to harm themself, take it seriously. Let them know that your most important job is to keep them safe, which means seeing a professional who helps children learn to cope with difficult feelings and experiences. You can call this hotline for immediate help if you can't quickly connect with a local therapist: National Parent Helpline: 1 (855) 427-2736.

WHEN YOUR CHILD IS NEGATIVE AND VENOMOUS TOWARD YOU

Most big reactors have been known to hurl their share of vitriol when they are, well, having big reactions. Some doozies include:

"Mommy, you are a toilet head!" and "Daddy, I am sending you back to the daddy store." They make some alarming threats and aggressive statements when they are angry or frustrated, like Violet (three and a half) who told her mom, Shelby, she could not be her mom anymore and that she was going to put her in a trash can, tie the lid on, and light it on fire. This was in response to Shelby sticking to the bedtime routine when Violet insisted that she had more feelings to talk about (after mom had already spent fifteen minutes cuddling and talking). Then there was Daniel (five), who hurled this vitriol when his dad, Alex, said it was time to stop playing to go inside for dinner: "You're the meanest daddy! You said we could play until it was dark and it's not even dark yet! I wish you weren't my daddy. I like Roger's daddy better." (*Note*: it was dark!)

While provocative statements and threats, especially coming from such a young child, feel so wrong, it's important not to interpret and react to these inflammatory exclamations at face value. Children don't always literally mean what they say. Your child is not a budding sociopath—as some parents worry. The stress from not getting something they want has activated their downstairs brain and they are purging emotion.

Your logical reaction might be that you need to teach your child a lesson through disciplinary action that shames or punishes them for this inappropriate outburst. But when you react harshly, it can escalate, rather than reduce, the distress that led your child to make the inappropriate proclamation to begin with. Big responses also reinforce unwanted behavior. So, when your child is mad at you for depriving them of something they desire, these provocative statements become effective strategies to get your attention and yank your chain, which results in more of these surly or "obnoxious" exclamations.

As counterintuitive as it may seem, what works is ignoring these unacceptable, troubling threats and accusations and, instead, giving voice to the underlying feeling your child is expressing. Shelby didn't react to Violet's threats to light her on fire, as disturbing as they were. She sat on the other side of the door playing some quiet music and worked on her laptop to distract herself. Within fifteen minutes, Violet calmed, asked Shelby to come in and kiss her goodnight, and said, "Mommy, I won't throw you in the trash and you can still be my mommy."

Daniel's dad, Alex, responded: "It's really hard to stop doing something that's so much fun. I don't like when we have to stop either." Then he went into the house and started helping with dinner. He resisted nagging Daniel to come inside. Within minutes Daniel went into the house on his own. Daniel then harumphed around, which Alex ignored. It was clear that Daniel was trying to get a reaction. Instead, Alex started talking to Daniel's mom about a movie they had recently watched together and purposefully recounted some parts incorrectly. That engaged Daniel—he had to set the record straight!—and they all successfully moved on.

And then there's this poignant story that powerfully illustrates that there's no one-size-fits-all approach. Toby and Stephen had come to see me for help with their son Lucas's (five) major meltdowns. They had made great progress. Then, they welcomed a new baby into the family. Lucas had a very hard time with this seismic change. He was expressing his confusion and anger by hurling horrible venom, especially at Toby and the baby. I had suggested addressing the underlying feelings at play. Here is what Toby reported about how that went and what actually worked: "We tried doing what you suggested. We stopped reprimanding Lucas for his hurtful words and didn't even react directly to them. I validated his feelings, but he just got angrier—shouting that he was not mad as he was raging. Then I stopped trying to do anything. I just looked at him calmly and quietly said, "Mm-hmm." It turns out that's what worked. He stopped and softened."

This story took my breath away. I was overcome by and in awe of Toby's incredible sensitivity and the self-control she had to resist getting reactive in the face of her child's attack. She was able to be Lucas' rock and not fuel his flame. This enabled her to take a step back and accept that none of the strategies, including mine, were working. She saw that using any language at all, even empathetic words, backfired in these moments. So, she pivoted and used what she was learning about Lucas—that less is almost always more in the heat of the moment—to come up with the most seemingly simple, sensitive solution. With minimal language and a calm and compassionate demeanor, she powerfully communicates to Lucas that she hears, sees, and accepts him, and that she is not afraid of his feelings—she can handle them. She gives Lucas exactly what he needs in those moments, which ends up reducing, not escalating, the unwanted and unhealthy language and behavior. This sensitive response enables them to maintain the connection Lucas so desperately needs right now. This is what attuned, "gentle parenting" looks like.

WHEN YOUR CHILD RESISTS REFLECTIVE DISCUSSIONS

One of the greatest gifts we give our children is self-awareness—a key component of emotional intelligence. Helping them understand what makes them tick—to tune in to and understand how their thoughts and feelings affect their behavior—is critical for their ability to develop effective, healthy ways to express their full range of emotions as they grow. It's also essential for developing strong, positive relationships.

Self-awareness is especially important for HSCs because of how deeply they register and react to their experiences in the world. Some HSCs are very open and eager to talk about their feelings after a meltdown or difficult incident has ended and they are calm. They often share profound and poignant insights, like the six-year-old who explained: "I remember them (the calming tools) before, and I remember them after. I just don't remember them in the middle." Or the five-year-old who said: "It's like the spirit leaves my body" after she's had an epic meltdown. Or the four-year-old who was able to tell her mom, who had recently just separated from her dad, that the reason she fights going to school every morning is because she's afraid mommy will disappear. As hard as it may be to hear our children share painful feelings, it's a positive sign that they have this insight and feel safe to share it with you. It also makes working through these difficult experiences possible.

But many parents I work with express concern about their children being resistant to talking about feelings. They refuse to engage in reflective discussions to process and learn from difficult incidents. They cover their ears, tell parents to go away, immediately change the subject, shout that they don't want to talk about it, or they make one of those alarming statements—like "I'm so stupid! I can't do anything right!"—to get you to back off. This reaction is rooted in the discomfort of revisiting an emotionally charged experience, especially when the child feels shame about it. The last thing they want is a face-to-face discussion that can feel very overwhelming, so they shut it down.

You can't, nor should you, try to force your kids to have these conversations. Pressuring them is intrusive and likely to result in digging in their heels more fiercely and redoubling their defenses. Further, they develop a knee-jerk, negative reaction every time you try to initiate these discussions, making it less likely they will feel safe to reflect and open up in the future.

Strategies to Reduce Defensiveness and Open Kids Up

Set a tone that is validating and doesn't convey any judgment or smack of being a correction. Your opening gambit is critical because it can make or break whether your child opens up or shuts down. If your tone is serious as you say something like "Let's talk about what happened at the playground today," or "Let's talk about your meltdown at the restaurant," your child is more likely to react defensively and shut down the discussion.

If, instead, you start with a statement that immediately communicates that you are not angry, disappointed, or judging them, but in fact, understand them, children are much more likely to be open to hearing what you have to say. "It was so disappointing when the restaurant didn't have your favorite dinosaur-shaped chicken nuggets. You were so upset that your body acted before your brain and you lost control. That happens. I understand."

Another strategy that can be very effective is to start a discussion that imposes new limits by telling your child that you are in trouble with their doctor.

Dr. Brooks was asking about how you were doing. We told her all about the new things you're learning. Then she asked about sleep, and we told her you were coming in and out of your room a lot and getting to bed late. She was upset with us because she said it's very unhealthy for kids not to get the sleep they need and it's our job as your dads to make sure you stay in your room after lights-out and get the sleep you need. We have to do a better job so here's the new plan.

Ask permission to share your thoughts. Children may be resistant to hearing our ideas because it feels overwhelming and intrusive. Asking for permission can be a game changer. Rather than launching in with your input, let them know you have some ideas for how to solve that problem and ask if they're interested in hearing them. I have seen this result in kids being much more open to parental input. "I have some ideas about why it's so hard and what you can do when you don't get what you want; when you're worried about joining in a new activity; and when your best friend decides to play with someone else at the playground."

If your child says they don't want to hear your input, accept it and let them know that you are happy to share your thoughts when they are ready. When you respect your child's boundaries, they are more likely to feel safe reflecting and sharing feelings down the road. They are much more likely to seek you out when they do want to talk. Remember, parenting is a marathon, not a race.

Be clear that your child doesn't have to say anything if they don't want to. "I have some ideas about why sometimes your body acts before your brain. Would you like to hear them? You can just listen. While I love hearing about your thoughts and feelings, you don't need to say anything—that's up to you." When we initiate these conversations, children may feel pressured by the inherent expectation that there is going to be some big tête-à-tête that requires them to share their thoughts and feelings when they may not be ready. Letting them know from the start that this is not your expectation can make them more open to listening to what you have to say.

Tell stories about yourself that mirror their experience. You might even come out of the gate by sharing your story and not even mentioning the incident. Bobby did this with her daughter, Nellie (four), who was very resistant to trying new activities. Nellie loves art and Bobby was pretty sure that Nellie would really enjoy an art class if she would take a risk and try it. Bobby shared the following story with her: "When I was a little girl, I loved to dance so my parents signed me up for a dance class. I was terrified and didn't want to go. I was afraid that I might not be good at it, that the teacher might be mean, and that I would feel uncomfortable with all the kids I didn't know. But my parents took me anyway. I was really angry and wouldn't participate for the first few classes, but then I saw how much fun it was, and I ended up loving it and making some new friends."

Nellie was fascinated by this story, asked Bobby a lot of questions about it, and begged her to tell the story over and over. Then Bobby asked Nellie if she ever felt this way—nervous about something—and if she had a story to tell about it. Nellie opened up in a way she had never done before. This led to a plan to observe an art class together so Nellie could check it out without having to participate. That first step ultimately led to Nellie joining and thriving in that same class.

Even if these stories don't result in kids opening up, it helps them see that they are not alone with their feelings and experiences and may make them more open to reflective discussions as they grow.

Make exploring and understanding feelings a fun activity. "I have some really interesting information to share, would you like to hear it?" If they say, "yes," continue: "Did you know that the words we say and what we do with our bodies all start with feelings? When I go to the refrigerator to get some food, it's because I'm feeling hungry, and my brain tells my body I need to eat! When I shout, it's because my brain is overwhelmed with really big feelings of frustration or anger."

Then introduce the idea of making a list of lots of different feelings. Talk about different ways those feelings might be expressed and what the outcomes might be. Start with examples they can easily identify with, like a child getting upset when a classmate takes some of the blocks they are playing with. What would the outcome be if the child hit the classmate with a block versus asking for help? What about when the restaurant doesn't have the kind of juice they want? What might be the outcome if they shout at the waiter versus taking a deep breath and being flexible by choosing a different drink? Exploring how feelings impact behavior through hypotheticals can open kids up to talking about their own feelings and behavior.

Read books that reflect the challenge you want to help your child with and use that to be "social detectives" together. Ask about:

- what they think the characters are thinking and feeling;
- why they might have acted as they did; how their thoughts and feelings affected their actions;
- what they might do differently to get a different outcome;

- if your child has ever felt like the characters in the book—whom they do and don't identify with and why; and
- if they have ever been in similar situations as any of the characters, what happened and what might they do differently to get a different outcome.

Offer alternative ways to communicate. You can schedule a video call (see detailed description of this strategy in chapter 2). Communicating in this way can also put kids in a more logical and open state of mind. They rise to being treated like a colleague. These "meetings" seem to work best when parents tell the child that they get to decide what issue to tackle first. Once they have a chance to share, kids are often more open to parents raising some issues. For example, Rose (four) said the issue she wanted to discuss was that there are never treats (sweets) in the school lunches her parents prepare for her. Her dad acknowledged Rose's disappointment. He also said they can't give her more treats than are healthy for her. She is allowed two each day. If she wants one at lunchtime, that's fine, but then there will be just one more at home, not two. She can choose to have the second one after school or after dinner. Her dad was amazed at how easily Rose accepted this and how satisfied she seemed to be. He attributed this to the meeting format. It made Rose feel grown up and more open to reason. Then it was his turn to raise an issue. He brought up Rose hitting when she is upset. He explained that he can't let her hit people because people have feelings and hitting hurts. He suggested they brainstorm ideas for other things she can do with her body when she is upset. They came up with a list of things she could safely hit. Since that meeting, while

Rose isn't always able to control herself, the hitting is less frequent, and when she does hit, she more easily accepts redirection.

You can also offer to share your thoughts in a voice recording. Your child can send their own recording with their feelings back. Or you can send an email and your child can write or dictate a reply. Of course, kids who aren't reading yet or who can't make their own voice recordings will need help. Using these "remote" vehicles is silly and fun. They create a lighthearted tone that cuts through the typical tension of these kinds of conversations, making kids less defensive and more open to sharing and reflecting. It also creates a safe distance between them and you that makes these conversations less emotionally charged, which can help kids be more logical and objective.

WHEN KIDS ARE SUPERSTARS AT SCHOOL AND "TERRORS" AT HOME

Eva's teachers report that she is one of the most cooperative and best helpers in the class. She's kind to her friends and is good at sharing. She's empathetic—always the first to comfort a peer who is struggling. In short, she's a total delight. At home it's a very different story. Eva is demanding. She ignores her parents' directions and melts down if she can't have what she wants when she wants it. Eva's parents are thrilled that she is doing so well in school. But they are perplexed and angry that she is so difficult at home when she clearly has the ability to show much greater self-control. They are at a loss for how to make sense of their Jekyll-and-Hyde daughter and how to get her to behave at home as she does in the classroom.

Multiple times a week, I talk with parents who report that their kids are superstars at school—calm, cooperative, and collaborative—but are "terrors" at home. They break down over seemingly minor issues, don't "listen," and are very inflexible and demanding.

A recent theory that is getting a lot of attention is that kids are "masking"—the term that has come to describe when people with ASD (autism spectrum disorder) try to act like their neurotypical peers in order to conform. Masking is detrimental because it's exhausting for kids to work so hard to adapt, and studies have shown that it can result in increased anxiety and depression.[1] Recently, this term is being more broadly applied to kids who exhibit this behavioral pattern and are not on the autistic spectrum, which has caused a lot of confusion for families. Based on my work with thousands of big reactors (some with ASD but most just highly sensitive) what I see, by and large, is that when kids do well at school, it's very positive, and not harmful, for kids. Teachers report and I observe that these kids don't look stressed or like automatons. They are regulated, positively engaged, energized, and happy. They are experiencing themselves as competent, well-liked human beings, which is a net positive.

There are many reasons why kids may behave quite differently at home and school. Tuning in to what the root cause might be for your child opens the door to responding in ways that can increase cooperation and reduce power struggles at home.

School is stressful. The stress kids experience as they learn to get along in a group is not harmful. It's considered "positive" stress (or "positive discomfort") because it leads to growth and the development of important new skills. This is happening in spades in early care and education settings. Think of the countless directions and rules children are expected to follow and the many transitions they need to make throughout what is often a very long day. And then there are the inevitable frustrations and disappointments that naturally arise in a group setting, such as not being the line-leader or the snack helper. This is a lot to manage for a young child whose "upstairs," thinking part of the brain, which is responsible for impulse control and self-regulation, is in the early stages of development. The mental and physical effort required to do what is expected at school is taxing. By the time they get home, kids are fried, like many of us after a long workday. They have left it all on the (classroom) table. This is especially true for highly sensitive kids who tend to be more intense and reactive by nature. They reach their threshold for managing typical life stressors sooner than more go-with-the-flow kids and, thus, are more likely to lose it at home after a long day at school.

School tends to be much more structured than home. In order to run a safe and calm classroom, teachers need to implement countless rules and provide secure boundaries. This lets the kids know exactly what to expect: enter class, put backpack in cubby, sit in circle (crisscross applesauce!), take a seat at the assigned space at the snack table, put the blocks in size order on the shelf, stop playing when the lights flick on and off, clean up when the clean-up song goes on, and so on. The directions and expectations are crystal clear, which is comforting to children. They know exactly what to expect, which helps them prepare for and cooperate with the many rules they have to follow.

For many families, the home environment is a completely different situation. Parents haven't had years of training on early childhood development and how to set clear limits in order to run an effective group setting (home is a group setting, too!). Parents are also more emotionally connected to and, therefore, reactive to their kids. The intensity of the parent–child relationship makes it harder to be clear and calm the way teachers can. Further, it's the teacher's job to be singularly focused on interacting with and guiding children. At home, parents are dealing with countless competing demands, including the dynamic between siblings, which can be very complicated and triggering for parents.

Young children know home is their safest place. Many of us are our best selves at work. We manage our emotions and reactivity. We are kind, cooperative, and communicate with warmth and respect. Then we get home and dump all our stress onto the people we care about and love the most. While this may not be healthy and is something many of us need to work on, we feel free to do it because we know, no matter what, our family will always accept and be there for us. The same is true for kids. Home is their safe space. It's because they trust you that they are free to fall apart with you.

Young children are testing out different roles. Because home is their safe space, it's also where kids are able to express themselves in ways they may not feel comfortable doing at school. Like Samir (four) who is very compliant at school. He is sensitive to the needs and feelings of others. He readily gives up toys to appease another child or surrenders his spot next to the teacher during circle time to a peer who is trying to squeeze her way into that space. At home, Samir feels freer to test out his power, to be more assertive. It may be in ways that are not acceptable, like demanding that his mom only read to him and not his little sister, but that's where setting loving limits come in.

What You Can Do

Don't take it personally! Your child isn't being defiant, nasty, or rejecting on purpose. They're just having a hard time coping. If you see their behavior as intentional, it puts you in a revved-up, negative state of mind that makes you more likely to fuel the flames, which begets more negativity and out-of-control behavior. What your child needs in these difficult moments is for you to be their rock, to acknowledge they are having a hard time, and to show them you can tolerate their distress. When your child says: "I am never going to wash my hands before dinner!" you might respond: "I know you don't want to stop playing but it's time to get ready for dinner. You have two great choices: you can pick any sink to wash your hands, or I can be a helper and use a wipe to get them clean before dinner." Most important is that you don't get drawn into a power struggle, which only increases stress.

Acknowledge and show empathy for how hard your child is working to be a good citizen at school. "We know it takes a lot of energy to follow all the rules, make so many transitions from one activity to another, and share and take turns with friends. That's a lot! By the time you get home you are really tired, which makes it hard to follow the rules at home. We understand."

Avoid making negative comparisons between your child's behavior at home and school. Instead of: "Ms. Tiffany says you are the best helper and listener at school. Why can't you do that at home?" Try: "You are doing such a great job following directions and being a good friend at school! That's awesome. Now we are going to work on how to help you follow directions at home, too. We know you can do it." You want to build on the positive. Taking a shaming approach increases negativity and leads to less, not more, cooperation.

Bake in time for connection upon reuniting. While this may seem impossible when your mind is on all the things that have to happen once everyone is home at the end of the day, the payoff can be big. Filling your child's (and your) cup after a long day apart can result in less overall stress and more cooperation. Creating a ritual can help a lot—even if it's just for ten or fifteen minutes. For example, read a chapter of a book as you cuddle together, or whatever special bonding activity you and your child enjoy. Connection is about the quality of the interaction, not the amount of time spent engaging. When your child can count on this ritual, it can reduce stress for everyone and result in more cooperation.

Scaffold for success. HSCs often need a break to refuel after school. Limit unnecessary demands or tasks that can be done once your child has had some downtime. Create a cozy corner in your home where they can chill out until they are ready to engage. It might include a kiddie tent, which can be very calming for kids. Fill it with cozy pillows and other calming items. This also might be the time you allow for screens, knowing this is zone-out time for your child. Recall the story of the mom who let her child have up to two hours of screen time after school, which resulted in a very calm and joyful mealtime and bedtime routine—well worth it for this family with an extremely intense, big reactor.

Keep in mind that if your child is thriving in a group setting, you should be giving yourself a good, strong pat on the back. It means you have given them the tools to get along in the real world: to be flexible, to tune in to others' ideas and needs, to wait their turn, and to effectively cope when something doesn't go their way. These are all skills children need to be effective in a group and that you have instilled in your child—you have given them the tools to thrive now and in the future!

Closing Thoughts

I hope the stories in this book have provided the validation you deserve for how daunting parenting a highly sensitive child can be and so you can see that you are not alone. I hope you also see that while it takes a heroic amount of patience and parental self-control to be the rock your child needs you to be, the payoff is huge. You are nurturing your glorious child's deep capacity for empathy, creativity, and insight, while also helping them manage their big emotions and reactions in order to successfully navigate life's ups and downs. There is no greater gift—to your child, yourself, and your family.

Resources

Autism Spectrum Disorder (ASD)

Understood: https://www.understood.org/

Attention-Deficit/Hyperactivity Disorder (ADHD)

ADDitude: https://www.additudemag.com/

Anxiety Disorders

Childmind Institute: https://childmind.org/

Early Brain Development

Beyond Behaviors: Using Brain Science and Compassion to Understand and Solve Children's Behavioral Challenges, by Mona Delahooke (PESI Publishing, 2019)

Explaining Brains: https://explainingbrains.com/

The Whole-Brain Child: Twelve Revolutionary Strategies to Nurture Your Child's Developing Mind, by Daniel J. Siegel and Tina Payne Bryson (Random House, 2011)

Early Intervention Services

"What You Need to Know: Early Intervention," by Rebecca Parlakian (ZERO TO THREE, 2018, https://bit.ly/34LR89S)

Highly Sensitive Children

The Explosive Child: A New Approach to Understanding and Parenting Easily Frustrated, Chronically Inflexible Children, by Ross Greene (Harper Paperbacks, 2021)

The Highly Sensitive Child: Helping Our Children Thrive When the World Overwhelms Them, by Elaine N. Aron (Harmony, 2002)

The Orchid and the Dandelion: Why Some Children Struggle and How All Can Thrive, by Thomas Boyce (Knopf, 2019).

Raising Your Spirited Child: A Guide for Parents Whose Child Is More Intense, Sensitive, Perceptive, Persistent, and Energetic, by Mary Sheedy Kurcinka (William Morrow Paperbacks, 2015)

Limit-Setting with Love/Parenting Without Power Struggles

Why Is My Child in Charge? A Roadmap to Increase Cooperation, Reduce Power Struggles, and Experience More Joy in Parenting, by Claire Lerner (Rowman & Littlefield, 2021)

Mealtime Challenges

Eat and Feed with Joy (Ellyn Satter): https://www.ellynsatterinstitute.org/

Sensory-based feeding challenges, SOS Approach to Feeding: https://sosapproachtofeeding.com/

Why Is My Child in Charge? A Roadmap to Increase Cooperation, Reduce Power Struggles, and Experience More Joy in Parenting

Safe Space Setup and Implementation

Why is My Child in Charge? A Roadmap to Increase Cooperation, Reduce Power Struggles, and Experience More Joy in Parenting

Sensory Processing Disorder (SPD)

The Out-of-sync Child: Recognizing and Coping With Sensory Processing Disorder, by Carol Stock Kranowitz (A Skylight Press Book/A Perigee Book, 2005)

Star Institute: https://www.spdstar.org/

Understood: https://www.understood.org/search-results/v1/search?query=sensory+processing

NOTES

Introduction

1. Ockwell-Smith, S. (n.d.). SO-S parenting with Sarah Ockwell-Smith. Retrieved June 1, 2024, from https://sarahockwell-smith.com/.
2. Bowlby, J. (1988). *A secure base: Parent-child attachment and healthy human development*. Basic Books.
3. Boyce, W. T. (2019). *The orchid and the dandelion: Why some children struggle and how all can thrive*. Knopf.
4. Lerner, C. (2022, February 21). Ten traits of highly sensitive children. *Psychology Today*. Retrieved June 20, 2024, from https://www.psychologytoday.com/us/blog/zero-to-six/202202/10-traits-of-highly-sensitive-children.
5. Boyce, W. T., & Ellis, B. J. (2005). Biological sensitivity to context: An evolutionary-developmental theory of the origins and functions of stress reactivity. *Development and Psychopathology*, *17*(2), 277–301 doi: 10.1017/s0954579405050145.

Chapter 1

1. Chess, S., & Thomas, A. (1984). *Origins and evolution of behavior disorders from infancy to early adulthood*. Brunner/Mazel.
2. Sulis, W. (2020). The continuum between temperament and mental illness as dynamical phases and transitions. *Frontiers in Psychiatry*, 11, 614982.
3. Acevedo, B. P., Jagiellowicz, J., Aron, E., Marhenke, R., & Aron, A. (2017). Sensory processing sensitivity and childhood quality's effects on neural responses to emotional stimuli. *Clinical Neuropsychiatry*, *14*(6), 359–373.'
4. Acevedo, B. P., Aron, E. N., Aron, A., Sangster, M. D., Collins, N., & Brown, L. L. (2014). The highly sensitive brain: An fMRI study of sensory

processing sensitivity and response to others' emotions. *Brain and Behavior*, 4(4), 580–594. doi: 10.1002/brb3.242.

5 Boyce, W. T. (2019). *The orchid and the dandelion: Why some children struggle and how all can thrive.* Knopf.

6 Boyce, W. T. (2016). Differential susceptibility of the developing brain to contextual adversity and stress. *Neuropsychopharmacology, 41*(1), 142–162. doi: 10.1038/npp.2015.294.

7 Lionetti, F., Aron, A., Aron, E. N., Burns, G. L., Jagiellowicz, J., & Pluess. M. (2018). Dandelions, tulips and orchids: evidence for the existence of low-sensitive, medium-sensitive and high-sensitive individuals. *Translational Psychiatry, 8*(1), 24. doi: 10.1038/s41398-017-0090-6.

8 Aron, E. N. (2002). *The highly sensitive child.* Harmony/Rodale. p. 30.

9 Wolf, M., van Doorn, G. S., & Weissing, F. J. (2008). Evolutionary emergence of responsive and unresponsive personalities. *Proceedings of the National Academy of Sciences, 105*(41), 15825–15830. https://doi.org/10.1073/pnas.0805473105.

10 Rodden, J. (2025, January 27). What is sensory processing disorder? *ADDitude*. Retrieved July 20, 2024, from https://www.additudemag.com/what-is-sensory-processing-disorder/.

11 Mental disorders. (2022, June 8). World Health Organization. Retrieved July 15, 2024, from https://www.who.int/news-room/fact-sheets/detail/mental-disorders#:~:text=A%20mental%20disorder%20is%20characterized,different%20types%20of%20mental%20disorders.

12 Aron, E., Allen-Williams, B., & Strickland, J. (2024). FAQ: Is sensory processing (or integration) disorder (SPD) the same as sensory processing sensitivity (SPS)? *The Highly Sensitive Person* (blog). https://hsperson.com/faq/spd-vs-sps/.

13 Belsky, G. (2023, December 4). Understanding sensory processing challenges. *Understood*. https://www.understood.org/en/articles/understanding-sensory-processing-challenges?utm_medium=cpc&utm_source=google-search-grant&utm_campaign=g_en_information_processing_challenges_lj&utm_content=spd&utm_term=sensory%20processing%20disorder_exact&g.

14 Acevedo, B. (2024, June 11). What is sensory processing sensitivity? Traits, insights, and ADHD Links. *ADDitude*. https://www.additudemag.com/highly-sensitive-person-sensory-processing-sensitivity-adhd/.

15 Hoogman, M., Bralten, J., Hibar, D. P., Mennes, M., Zwiers, M. P., Schweren, L. S. J., van Hulzen, K. J. E., Medland, S. E., Shumskaya, E., Jahanshad, N., Zeeuw, P., Szekely, E., Sudre, G., Wolfers, T., Onnink, A. M. H., Dammers, J. T., Mostert, J. C., Vives-Gilabert, Y., Kohls, G., . . . Franke, B. (2017). Subcortical brain volume differences in participants with attention deficit hyperactivity disorder in children and adults: A cross-sectional mega-analysis. *Lancet Psychiatry, 4*(4), 310–319. doi: 10.1016/S2215-0366(17)30049-4.

16 Acevedo, B., Aron, E., Pospos, S., & Jessen, D. (2018). The functional highly sensitive brain: A Review of the brain circuits underlying sensory processing sensitivity and seemingly related disorders. *Philosophy Transactions of the Royal Society B, 373*(1744), 20170161. doi: 10.1098/rstb.2017.0161.

17 Rudy, L. J. (2024, October 9). Understanding the three levels of autism. *Very Well Health*. https://www.verywellhealth.com/what-are-the-three-levels-of-autism-260233.

18 Acevedo, Aron, Pospos, & Jessen, The functional highly sensitive brain.

19 Aron, *The highly sensitive child*, p. 30.

Chapter 2

1 Siegel, D. J., & Bryson, T. P. (2012). *The whole-brain child*. Random House.

2 Ainsworth, M. D. S., Blehar, M. C., Waters, E., & Wall, S. (1978). *Patterns of attachment: A psychological study of the strange situation*. Lawrence Erlbaum Associates.

Chapter 3

1 Miller, C. (2025, February 10). Pathological demand avoidance in kids. Child Mind Institute. Retrieved October 22, 2024, from https://childmind.org/article/pathological-demand-avoidance-in-kids/.

2 Bates, R. A., Militello, L., Barker, E., Villasanti, H. G., & Schmeer, K. (2022). Early childhood stress responses to psychosocial stressors: The state of the science. *Developmental Psychobiology, 64*(7), e22320. doi: 10.1002/dev.22320.

Chapter 4

1 Toxic stress. (n.d.). Center on the Developing Child, Harvard University. Retrieved July 9, 2024, from https://developingchild.harvard.edu/science/key-concepts/toxic-stress/.

2 Porges, S. W. (2011). *The polyvagal theory: Neurophysiological foundations of emotions, attachment, communication, and self-regulation.* W. W. Norton & Company.

Chapter 5

1 Aron, E. (1998). *The highly sensitive person: How to thrive when the world overwhelms you.* Three Rivers Press.

2 Toxic stress. (n.d.). Center on the Developing Child, Harvard University. Retrieved July 9, 2024, from https://developingchild.harvard.edu/science/key-concepts/toxic-stress/.

3 Eisenberg, N., Spinrad, T. L., & Eggum, N. D. (2010). Emotion-related self-regulation and its relation to children's maladjustment. *Annual Review of Clinical Psychology, 6*, 495–525.

Chapter 7

1 Lionetti, F., Pastore, M., & Barone, L. (2015). Sensitivity to the environment and its impact on social development. *Developmental Psychology Review, 25*, 1–22.

2 Obama, M. (2018). *Becoming*. Crown Publishing Group.

3 Winner, M. G., & Crooke, P. J. (2008). *You are a social detective: Explaining social thinking to kids*. Social Thinking Publishing.

Chapter 8

1 Masking. (n.d.). National Autistic Society. Retrieved July 10, 2025, from https://www.autism.org.uk/advice-and-guidance/topics/behaviour/masking.

REFERENCES

Acevedo, B., Aron, E., Pospos, S., & Jessen, D. (2018). The functional highly sensitive brain: A Review of the brain circuits underlying sensory processing sensitivity and seemingly related disorders. *Philosophy Transactions of the Royal Society B, 373*(1744), 20170161. doi: 10.1098/rstb.2017.0161.

Acevedo, B. (2024, June 11). What is sensory processing sensitivity? Traits, insights, and ADHD Links. *ADDitude.* https://www.additudemag.com/highly-sensitive-person-sensory-processing-sensitivity-adhd/.

Acevedo, B. P., Jagiellowicz, J., Aron, E., Marhenke, R., & Aron, A. (2017). Sensory processing sensitivity and childhood quality's effects on neural responses to emotional stimuli. *Clinical Neuropsychiatry, 14*(6), 359–373.

Acevedo, B. P., Aron, E. N., Aron, A., Sangster, M. D., Collins, N., & Brown, L. L. (2014). The highly sensitive brain: An fMRI study of sensory processing sensitivity and response to others' emotions. *Brain and Behavior 4*(4), 580–594. doi: 10.1002/brb3.242.

Ainsworth, M. D. S., Blehar, M. C., Waters, E., & Wall, S. (1978). *Patterns of attachment: A psychological study of the strange situation.* Lawrence Erlbaum Associates.

Aron, E. (1998). *The highly sensitive person: How to thrive when the world overwhelms you.* Three Rivers Press.

Aron, E. N. (2002). *The highly sensitive child: Helping our children thrive when the world overwhelms them.* Harmony.

Aron, E., Allen-Williams, B., & Strickland, J. (2024). FAQ: Is sensory processing (or integration) disorder (SPD) the same as sensory processing sensitivity (SPS)? *The Highly Sensitive Person* (blog). https://hsperson.com/faq/spd-vs-sps/.

Bates, R. A., Militello, L., Barker, E., Villasanti, H. G., & Schmeer, K. (2022). Early childhood stress responses to psychosocial stressors: The state of the science. *Developmental Psychobiology, 64*(7), e22320. doi: 10.1002/dev.22320.

Belsky, G. (2023, December 4). Understanding sensory processing challenges. *Understood.* https://www.understood.org/en/articles/understanding-sensory-processing-challenges?utm_medium=cpc&utm_source=google-search-grant&utm_campaign=g_en_information_processing_challenges_lj&utm_content=spd&utm_term=sensory%20processing%20disorder_exact&g.

Bowlby, J. (1988). *A secure base: Parent-child attachment and healthy human development.* Basic Books.

Boyce, W. T. (2016). Differential susceptibility of the developing brain to contextual adversity and stress. *Neuropsychopharmacology, 41*(1), 142–162. doi: 10.1038/npp.2015.294.

Boyce, W. T. (2019). *The orchid and the dandelion: Why some children struggle and how all can thrive.* Knopf.

Boyce, W. T., & Ellis, B. J. (2005). Biological sensitivity to context: An evolutionary-developmental theory of the origins and functions of stress reactivity. *Development and Psychopathology, 17*(2), 277–301. doi: 10.1017/s0954579405050145.

Chess, S., & Thomas, A. (1984). *Origins and evolution of behavior disorders from infancy to early adulthood.* Brunner/Mazel.

Eisenberg, N., Spinrad, T. L., & Eggum, N. D. (2010). Emotion-related self-regulation and its relation to children's maladjustment. *Annual Review of Clinical Psychology, 6,* 495–525.

Hoogman, M., Bralten, J., Hibar, D. P., Mennes, M., Zwiers, M. P., Schweren, L. S. J., van Hulzen, K. J. E., Medland, S. E., Shumskaya, E., Jahanshad, N., Zeeuw, P., Szekely, E., Sudre, G., Wolfers, T., Onnink, A. M. H., Dammers, J. T., Mostert, J. C., Vives-Gilabert, Y., Kohls, G., . . . Franke, B. (2017). Subcortical brain volume differences in participants with attention deficit hyperactivity disorder in children and adults: A cross-sectional mega-analysis. *Lancet Psychiatry, 4*(4), 310–319. doi: 10.1016/S2215-0366(17)30049-4.

Lerner, C. (2022, February 21). Ten traits of highly sensitive children. *Psychology Today.* Retrieved June 20, 2024, from https://www.psychologytoday.com/us/blog/zero-to-six/202202/10-traits-of-highly-sensitive-children.

Lionetti, F., Aron, A., Aron, E. N., Burns, G. L., Jagiellowicz, J., & Pluess. M. (2018). Dandelions, tulips and orchids: evidence for the existence of low-sensitive, medium-sensitive and high-sensitive individuals. *Translational Psychiatry, 8*(1), 24. doi: 10.1038/s41398-017-0090-6.

Lionetti, F., Pastore, M., & Barone, L. (2015). Sensitivity to the environment and its impact on social development. *Developmental Psychology Review, 25,* 1–22.

Masking. (n.d.). National Autistic Society. Retrieved July 10, 2025, from https://www.autism.org.uk/advice-and-guidance/topics/behaviour/masking.

Mental disorders. (2022, June 8). World Health Organization. Retrieved July 15, 2024, from https://www.who.int/news-room/fact-sheets/detail/mental-disorders#:~:text=A%20mental%20disorder%20is%20characterized,different%20types%20of%20mental%20disorders.

Miller, C. (2025, February 10). Pathological demand avoidance in kids. Child Mind Institute. Retrieved October 22, 2024, from https://childmind.org/article/pathological-demand-avoidance-in-kids/.

Obama, M. (2018). *Becoming.* Crown Publishing Group.

Ockwell-Smith, S. (n.d.). SO-S parenting with Sarah Ockwell-Smith. Retrieved June 1, 2024, from https://sarahockwell-smith.com/.

Porges, S. W. (2011). *The polyvagal theory: Neurophysiological foundations of emotions, attachment, communication, and self-regulation.* W. W. Norton & Company.

Rodden, J. (2025, January 27). What is sensory processing disorder? *ADDitude.* Retrieved July 20, 2024, from https://www.additudemag.com/what-is-sensory-processing-disorder/.

Rudy, L. J. (2024, October 9). Understanding the three levels of autism. *Very Well Health.* https://www.verywellhealth.com/what-are-the-three-levels-of-autism-260233.

Siegel, D. J., & Bryson, T. P. (2012). *The whole-brain child.* Random House.

Sulis, W. (2020). The continuum between temperament and mental illness as dynamical phases and transitions. *Frontiers in Psychiatry,* 11, 614982.

Toxic stress. (n.d.). Center on the Developing Child, Harvard University. Retrieved July 9, 2024, from https://developingchild.harvard.edu/science/key-concepts/toxic-stress/.

Winner, M. G., & Crooke, P. J. (2008). *You are a social detective: Explaining social thinking to kids.* Social Thinking Publishing.

Wolf, M., van Doorn, G. S., & Weissing, F. J. (2008). Evolutionary emergence of responsive and unresponsive personalities. *Proceedings of the National Academy of Sciences,* 105(41), 15825–15830. https://doi.org/10.1073/pnas.0805473105.

ACKNOWLEDGMENTS

To the families who have allowed me into their hearts, minds, and homes to partner with them to be sensitive, loving parents to their big reactors: I have learned so much from you that has strengthened my ability to support other families. I am in awe of your resilience and how hard you are working to be the rock your children need you to be.

To my agent, Joelle Delbourgo, and editor, Christen Karniski, who recognized and appreciated the need to support families in the trenches with these amazing and fierce kids, and who believed in the power of these stories to provide meaningful support to families with big reactors.

To Lesli Rotenberg, who serves double duty as beloved friend and excellent editor: You are the most patient and attuned listener. Your thoughtful questions have brought clarity to these pages. I am so appreciative of your generosity in taking the time out of your busy days to read this entire book. Having you by my side to work out all things personal and professional, and serving as my personal yogi, has enriched my life so deeply.

To Renee Lerner, my amazing mom who, at eighty-nine, still has the sharpest of minds and continues to serve as my most committed editor and fiercest supporter: I am so grateful for the time you took to read every word in this book, for your meticulous attention to detail, and for your wisdom and guidance. I feel so lucky to have a mom who is such a strong role model and true collaborator and friend.

To my son, Sam, who helped me learn many of the lessons that are embedded throughout this book—about the awesomeness of highly sensitive children and what they need from their parents to thrive: I delight in your passion, charisma, and creativity. I am so grateful for the bond we share and how our relationship keeps growing and strengthening. I treasure our deep connection that is so fortifying for me.

To my daughter, Jess, who reviewed early chapters and helped me think through some foundational questions that set me off on the right course: Jess, you always help me see things from new perspectives and push me to refine my thinking. I am so appreciative of how seriously you value my work and the wisdom you share that always makes it better. I feel so lucky to have your love, support, and partnership, and most of all our close connection that feeds my soul.

Last and most definitely not least, to my husband, Rich, the dandelion to my orchid, and my much-needed rock: I am so grateful for your steady support and for always helping me find clarity, in dealing with life's challenges and now in my writing. Your incisive mind and exacting standards have made this book stronger. I also don't know how I would have gotten through this process without the levity and laughter you create in our home that provides so much joy and relief from the stress of working full time while also writing this book. I could not have done it without your humor, support, and partnership.

INDEX

Note: Several key topics are not listed in this index as they are addressed in nearly every page and story in this book: temperament, limit-setting/discipline, preventing power struggles, shame, meltdowns/tantrums, child parental self-regulation, inflexibility need for control, problem-solving and building resilience.

adhd   24–5
   definition   24
   difference from high sensitivity   24–5
aggression
   physical   63–7, 70, 177, 224, 227, 230
   verbal   40, 247–9
anxiety   117–36
   avoidance   118–20, 122, 127
   cautious and slow-to-warm   17–18, 137–65
   difference from high sensitivity   29–30
   exposure   120, 125, 127, 130–3
   fear of being alone   134
   hesitance to try new things   137
   separation anxiety   50–1, 57–63, 134
   surprises/unexpected   21, 63–4, 84–6, 129, 133
   when to seek professional help   136
   worry thinking brain   58, 125, 131, 134–5, 149–50
apologizing
   kids saying sorry   189–91, 218
   parents saying sorry   96

attachment   55–6 (*see also* separation anxiety)
autism spectrum disorder (ASD)   25–9
   definition   26
   difference from high sensitivity   25–9

brain development
   "downstairs" brain   40, 247
   upstairs brain   258
   worry vs thinking brain   58, 125, 131, 134–5, 149–50

cautious and slow-to-warm   17–18, 137–65
   adapting to school   155–61
   birthday parties   34, 161–2
   cheerleading/coaxing   142–3, 147
   hesitant to try something new   141–2, 142–54, 163–4

dandelions   3, 14, 82, 165
demand avoidance   86–7, 202

Elaine Aron   14, 138
emotional support parents   34–9, 41–2, 49–50, 96

INDEX

empathy
  capacity for 15, 16, 25, 26, 180
  concern for lack of 189, 216, 217–19
  for the child 4, 36, 49, 61, 78, 94, 106, 109, 178, 185, 197, 202, 213, 218, 235, 245, 260
  towards siblings 222, 235

four-year-olds
  anxiety 122–8
  bedtime battles 76–7
  being controlling 194
  hesitant to try new things 163–4, 253–4
  inflexibility 107–8
  intolerance of being corrected 187–8
  negative self-talk 240–1
  superstar at school and "terror" at home 259

five-year-olds
  avoidance of new experiences 144–55, 161–3
  demand for constant attention 31–2, 68–72
  fears 129–33
  hurling vitriol 40, 247
  opposition 140
  perfectionism 172–6
  quick to shame 180–6
  sibling jealousy 248–9
  social challenges 200–6

gentle parenting 1–5, 45–8, 63

intolerant of corrections 19, 169, 171, 180–6, 187–8, 217

lying 181, 185

masking 257

negative self-talk 182, 184, 239–46,

orchids 13, 14, 165

parental preferences 50–7, 76–7, 233–4, 236
parental self-regulation
  co-parenting 36, 53–6
  kids being aggressive 63–7, 70
  need for breaks 45
  not rescuing 36–9, 40, 42, 46, 170
peer relationships 193–221
  being "mean" 193, 196–7, 206–12, 213
  being "social detectives" 203, 210, 214, 216
  collaborating with teachers 205, 212–15
  competitiveness 194–5
  controlling/bossy 194, 206, 207, 208
  difficulty collaborating 195
  effective parenting approaches 202–5, 208–11, 214
  exclusion 196, 212–15
  insecurity 197–8, 207, 216
  reasons for social challenges 193–6
  rejection 200–6, 212–13
  self-consciousness 194
  teasing 195, 200, 106, 215, 216
  when to seek help 196, 220–1
perfectionism 168–9, 170, 172–6, 182–6
praise
  problem with overpraising 209

when kids reject it 20, 119, 122–8, 146, 172–5

safe space breaks 45, 70, 226–9, 232, 236
screens 71, 100
self-consciousness 19, 20, 146, 178, 188
   avoidance 118, 150–1
   peer challenges 194
   perfectionism 19, 20, 154–5
   praise 126
separation anxiety 50–1, 57–63
sensory processing
   definition 22
   difference from high sensitivity 22–4
   impact of 33, 84
seven-year-olds
   being excluded 212–15
   demanding all attention 232–7
   fear of being alone 134
   irritability 42–3, 78–9
   sass 111–14
   screen time 43–4
   self-regulation 47–8
   social challenges 188–91
   sore losing 167, 177–80
sibling relationship 221–37
   building empathy 235–6
   effective parenting approaches 225–31
   jealousy 248–9
   limit-setting 233, 234, 226–7
   monopolizing attention 232–7
   problem-solving 227–8, 230
   refereeing 229
   sharing 228
   teasing 224
six-year-olds
   bedtime struggles 73, 245–6
   being bossy 206–12
   intense reactions 91–104
   irrational demands 108–11
   negative self-talk 240, 241
   separation anxiety 50–63
   sibling conflict 224–32
   social anxiety 196
sleep (bedtime)
   delaying 38
   parental preference 236
   power struggles 16–17, 76–7, 90
   setting limits 38, 73–4, 111–14, 245–6
sore losing 169–70, 177–80, 209

three-year-olds
   anxiety at starting school 155–61
   bedtime struggles 247
   dependence on emotional support parent 36–7
   fear of the unknown 133–4
   inflexibility 23, 63–7
   intense sensory reactions 34
   keen insight 15
transitions 21, 63–4, 84–6
two-year-olds
   inflexibility 104–7

ABOUT THE AUTHOR

Claire Lerner is a licensed clinical social worker and child development specialist and the author of *Why Is My Child in Charge? A Roadmap to Ending Power Struggles, Increasing Cooperation, and Finding Joy in Parenting Young Children* (Rowman & Littlefield, 2021). She served as the director of parenting resources at ZERO TO THREE for eighteen years where she translated the science of early childhood for parents and professionals. Claire has also been a practicing clinician for more than thirty-five years, partnering with parents to do the detective work of decoding their children's behavior to solve their most vexing childrearing challenges. She also provides training and consultation to preschools and pediatric residents at Children's National Medical Center. Claire is the author of hundreds of parenting resources, including books, blogs, podcasts, and videos. She has served as a content expert for numerous national daily newspapers. Claire is the mother of two very spirited children, Sam (thirty-four) and Jess (thirty-two), and two stepchildren, Justin (thirty-four) and Sammy (thirty-one). She lives in Bethany Beach, Delaware, with her husband, Rich, and their beloved Golden, Hudson.